Still Wearing

Double-

Breasted

Suits

A Breast Cancer Survivor's Story

By
Cheryl S. Fisher

This book is dedicated to my remarkable medical team:
Dr. David Powell, Dr. Tariq Sheikh, Dr. David Neidhardt,
Dr. Sarah Olt, Dr. Rena Zimmerman, and Dr. Frederick
Ferri, and their staffs of medical professionals.

© 2006 by Cheryl S. Fisher
All Rights Reserved

ISBN 1-59872-648-X
Printed in the United States of America

No portion of this publication may be reproduced, stored in or introduced into
a retrieval system, or transmitted in any form or in any manner, (electronic,
mechanical, photocopying, recording, or otherwise) without prior written
permission from the author, except for short quotations in reviews or essays.

Third Printing
This edition was produced and published by:
Peck Publishing
2280 N. Glenwood Ave.
Lima, Ohio 45805

For E-mail orders: csfbiz@woh.rr.com

"Having cancer is like
   waiting for the other shoe
      to drop
      and finding you live
      downstairs from a centipede."

I can't claim this statement as my own. Its original author is now unknown to me, but I have made its application to cancer.

Table of Contents

How Do You Counteract It?
Is It Hot In Here? I Can't Sleep!
Chemo-Brain

Dr. Powell's Staff
The First Sign of Improvement
Meals on Wheels
"Is This Good?"
Does Anything Taste Good?
More Family On the Move
The Third Move is Completed
Girls Just Gotta Have Fun
Scrappin' the Poetry
No Lights, No Furnace
Pneumonia
Power Up!
Just Because You're Paranoid Doesn't Mean They're Not After You!
Dr. Powell Selects Another Drug
What Is Next?
Bretta and the Family
Cut it Short... No, Give Me a Buzz!
Hats Off!
The Photo Shoot
Wigs
More of Sarah's Shenanigans
'Cat' Scan, 'Dolphin' Scan, PET Scan
Grammie and the Baby
"It's Like Getting My Own Baby Back"
The Therapeutic Baby
And Then There Were Two
Talking About It
I'm Clever, Even Under Anesthesia
Another Liver Biopsy
Will the News Be Good?
The Finish Line is In Sight!
Here I Go, Thinking Again

5

Note: Throughout the book you will find sections called, "From my Journal." These are selected entries from a journal that I kept during this illness. The first of these entries is on page 11.

6

Acknowledgements

Many thanks are owed to my miracle-producing team of medical marvels (See Dedication). Also to our numerous friends who provided such tremendous support throughout this ordeal. Many of you expressed your love and concern to my family members when you didn't see me, and those sentiments were relayed to me faithfully.

The numerous staff members at St. Rita's Medical Center with whom I came in contact since that day in February 2004 have my admiration and deepest respect. I was treated with the greatest respect and dignity, and though I am unable to thank each of you here individually, I should have at the time! Your kind faces and professional skill will always be remembered. I was already acquainted with many of you through my work, but it leaves a much deeper impression when you are **in** the bed instead of **beside** it!

My grateful thanks go also to the woman who gave me life, my mother, Bernice LaViness. She and my father Melvin, provided my sisters and me with the most delightful childhood in a home full of love. She made me the woman I am today. Mom has been by my side through all of this, having moved here from her 21-year residence in Florida. She still calls me her "baby" and as the last of her children, I qualify for that designation!

To my daughter Angie Horn, thanks for being the levelheaded one that could call to mind whatever bit of information the chemo and Percocet made me forget! Your sharp mind and quick wit never fail to amuse me. Thank you also for sitting with Dad during all those CT scans and assisting with editing this project.

To my daughter Christy Martinez, thanks for disrupting your life and the lives of your little family to be nearer to me during this time. That was a sacrifice I will never forget. Besides, while you were staying here and commuting to Columbus on weekends, it was almost like old times having you home again! Thank you, too, for your expertise with the computer in preparing this project for the publisher.

To my son Mark, thank you for "taking charge" when all the girls were falling apart emotionally. You helped them to see that there really *was* something they could do even if they could not make me well themselves. You showed us all what being a man is about. Your strength helped me through many dark days and I hope there will be more opportunities to observe that strength in the future.

And to *my* baby Sarah Smith, thank you for your hugs and tears, for doing my nails, for vacuuming every week, for making me laugh when no one else could and for making life fun again. Memories of the no-hat trip to Wal-Mart and the "photo shoot" will always bring a smile to my face!! Never underestimate the value of your presence.

To my soul-mate and mother of Mark's children, Natalie, thank you for the late night 'girl-talks,' for watching movies with me, taking me shopping, and for all of your help here at home. We never knew we would be so close and at least from my perspective, it has only made me love you more. Mark always said we were a lot alike and he was right about that. I will be *eternally* grateful to you for those beautiful girls and your warm companionship! You have become our fourth daughter!

To my sister Ardy Fark, thanks for sharing the joy of Gershwin with me and for all your encouraging visits. Knowing you've seen some of the worst of this disease and its effects, just having you here meant so much. It's good having you so close.

To my sister Karen Norris, thank you for your frequent visits and phone calls. As the only one left in the LaViness family who is still gainfully employed your time has been limited somewhat, but not your expressions of love and joy over every tiny bit of progress attained. How I have treasured every moment with you!

To my niece Missie Norris, thank you for your visits and e-mails, your avid participation in Montgomery County's "Relay for Life" and

8

your warm support. Seeing the list of names above it's easy to see that this kind of expression is "in the blood" but you give "family" a new meaning! And thanks (to you and your mom) for introducing all of us to scrap booking!

Most of all to my dear, faithful husband **Earl**, thanks for everything. You cooked, cleaned, did laundry, ran to the pharmacy, carried my purse (Yes, he did!), showered me with gifts, gave updates to family and friends, paid the bills, drove me to countless appointments for 21 months- day and night- when I couldn't drive myself, told me what I needed to know from the newspaper so I wouldn't waste my time reading the whole thing, laughed with me, cried with me, kept me focused on what was important for each day, made me lie down when I didn't have enough sense to do so, brought me Percocet and water when I went to bed *before* remembering that I needed it one more time, held my hand and my heart, and went with me for all of those chemo treatments! Through all of that you held us all together spiritually, continuing to keep up with your privileges as an elder in our local congregation of Jehovah's Witnesses. You carried on when many men would have been carried out!
Other than that, you weren't very busy!

We stood up together 40 years ago and said, "…in sickness and in health…" For nearly two years you endured the "sickness" part with your silent strength and kept me from falling apart completely. I hope that the "health" part follows, and because of the medical marvels we have had in our midst, it just might be possible. I love you, now and forever!

Disclaimer

Nearly every product today has a disclaimer. Here's mine:

The events about which you will soon read are true to the best of my recollection from a brain clouded by nineteen months of chemotherapy and use of controlled substances.

That said, I admit that minor details may or may not be precisely correct. If, however, I am able to hold your attention to the end, you will learn that this complicated disease we call cancer can be overcome, and that there are indeed some dedicated physicians out there who care about their patients and work hard toward their recovery.

You must also realize that just as virtually every person in the world is a unique individual, no two people given the same diagnosis will have exactly the same treatment, even from the same doctor. Nor will their outcomes be the same. So if your aunt or your sister, your mom or your grandmother had breast cancer, her story will be far different from mine.

What is common to cancer patients is that they all know what it means to submit to the often devastating treatments that they hope will bring some relief from this disease. Most likely, the illness crept in silently with little or no evidence that it was even there until one day when its host said, "I've *got* to see the doctor about this!" Perhaps it was a cough or a pain that wouldn't go away. In any case if you have some symptom that just doesn't improve, no matter how insignificant it may seem to you, *get it checked out!*

Cancer is very treatable today, especially when detected early enough, and more therapies are being discovered as this story goes to press. Find out what's wrong, assemble a team of physicians who truly care, share your hopes, joys, sorrows and disappointments with *someone,* and *never lose hope.* In addition, if you haven't already, search for God who gives comfort to depressed souls. (See 2 Corinthians1:3, 4)

So, what ever you or someone you love may be facing, "...Be of good courage and say, 'Jehovah is my helper; I will not be afraid. What can man do to me?'" Hebrews 13:6

Foreword

Surely you know someone who has or had cancer. It's nearly impossible not to. There are 185,000 new cases of breast cancer every year in this country. Someone once said it's like being a member of a club you didn't want to join. You become instantly, inextricably linked to many other individuals who also didn't join this club voluntarily. People you might have not even met under other circumstances. Without a word spoken, without any explanations, you both know something of what the other has endured.

It changes your life forever. You will never look casually at a sunrise or sunset again. Or your family or a flower, a baby, a pet, a mountain, or the ocean. Instead, you will linger a few moments longer to enjoy each one more. You will want to lock them away in your memory. Cancer makes one aware of how fragile life is.

So this is the story of my battle with breast cancer. Why should another story be told? Because each one is unique and when the battle is won against the odds, the telling of it may give one other person the courage to face their own battle.

My first real clue that something was wrong was pain. Which takes me back to the days when my eldest daughter was perhaps twelve years old or so. She had a stomachache. Since I am a nurse, she had always heard conversations about this illness or that and was used to being questioned when she did not feel well.

"Do you hurt somewhere?... Where do you hurt?... Do you feel feverish?"

So on this particular occasion we had ruled out several things. She was not nauseated, had no fever, sore throat or earache.

"Do you think I have cancer?" she asked, desiring a reason for the way she was feeling. The expression on her face was clearly one of worry.

"No, dear. Don't be silly. Pain is the LAST symptom of cancer!" I replied, thinking that would relieve her of *that* thought.

"Oh, *no!*" she cried with all the drama she could muster, "I'm *dyyyying!*"

Well, that little illness was overcome shortly, but the statement remains true. Pain is one of the last symptoms of cancer. Unfortunately, by then it has often invaded one's body to the point that it becomes very difficult, if not impossible to arrest.

I was diagnosed with Stage IV breast cancer, meaning it had already spread to a distant organ. I knew my chances for survival were slim (perhaps only 20%), and so did most of my family and friends.

As you read what follows, you will see that this illness appeared in spite of my having done all the seemingly "right" things and was indeed overcome against all odds. I faced this illness with determination to take one day at a time. How else can you live?

I decided I would deal with each facet of this illness as it came. I tried not to look too far into the future, either for good or for bad.

Every day I prayed for courage, strength and endurance, and those prayers were answered. I found that with the strength imparted by my faith in Jehovah God and the love of my family and friends, I could fight this disease. The bonus is that I also survived and, for the time being, I have won the fight. I am cancer free and in remission! Not only that, but I still have both of my breasts! Thus the title of this book.

Chapter 1

"What's That White Spot?"

The pain made me wince and nearly double over, grabbing my side with my right arm as though I were clutching an invisible football. It was up under my ribs on the right side, just above the waist. There was also pain in my back, below the right shoulder blade. On a scale of one to ten –as a nurse I always required that my patients quantify their pain- it was at least a six. I always reserve eight or nine for childbirth, which I have experienced four times, and ten for a gallstone in the common duct, which I experienced once.

It was early January 2004. I didn't have time for this, I thought as I continued working from my tall computer chair in the hallway of the 450-bed hospital where I worked. After nearly 21 years of hands on, direct patient contact nursing, I had a rather cushy job. It's called Utilization Review, something I never really understood until I was trained for the position. It involves reviewing the patients' charts, and evaluating the medical necessity, efficiency, and appropriateness of health care services and treatment plans, then communicating this information to the appropriate insurance company.

The hospital had applied for "Magnet" status and everyone had been abuzz for months now with what was necessary to meet the proper requirements. If all efforts were successful the achievement of Magnet status would enhance the institution's prestige. That year there were only a handful of medical centers in the nation that had that elite designation. The official visit for evaluation by the "Magnet" team was next week and there was no time for anyone to have extra days off.

But the pain was impossible to ignore. It lasted intermittently about two days and when the pain was no longer severe, I felt as though someone had kicked me in the ribs. I was left with a dull ache and an unusual feeling of fullness in that area. Mostly it was a conscious awareness of a part of my body that I could normally ignore. I knew that was the location of my liver. What I didn't know was why it hurt.

So I delayed for several days making an appointment to see my family doctor.

A Visit to the Doctor

I have since read that the average length of time between the appearance of the first symptoms of cancer and the first visit to a doctor is three months. If I had waited that long, someone else might be telling this story with a much different ending.

The appointment was within a few days of my call. The visit seemed rather ordinary. I described the pain. There was nothing else, no nausea, no vomiting, no fever or jaundice, no unexplainable weight loss or gain, no other pain.

Dr. Neidhardt (pronounced NIDE-heart) has been our family practitioner for more than ten years. He is about average height and is quite trim, almost boyish in appearance though his hair is graying slightly.

He gives thoughtful consideration to our every need and we never feel rushed in our visits. At the same time he runs a tight ship. By that I mean that, barring the random office disaster, such as a cardiac arrest in the office or the patient who calls reporting one problem and then wants to discuss seven of them, *he works on schedule!* If my appointment is at 10:00, I can arrive at 9:55 and be on my way home by 10:20 or so. We find that to be a medical miracle, one that amazes people who are not his patients!

"We'll get some blood work," he said after his examination, "and an ultrasound of the liver." His voice was as calm as usual, his words measured. His nurse would schedule these tests and call me.

Dr. Neidhardt ordered a hepatic (liver) function panel and the liver ultrasound.

The voice on the phone in the Radiology department informed me that the liver ultrasound would take about twenty minutes. I planned on using the time for my lunch break to have the test done and eating at my desk while I faxed insurance companies later.

"I'll Be Back in 20 Minutes" ...Right!

That morning I had to delay breakfast until after the blood was drawn for the liver function panel. This particular blood test required that I be "fasting" for at least 8 hours. So when the time came I left my desk and told my companion I'd be back in 20 minutes or so. The blood was drawn easily by one of the laboratory staff members and I proceeded to the Radiology department. After a brief wait I was called. I undressed from the waist up as instructed, and put the gown on.

I settled onto the cart and the area around my liver was exposed by the tech. The gel for the ultrasound probe felt warm. That's nice, I thought. It used to always be cold - room temperature, but still a shock to skin that's normally warm and covered by clothing. The room was darkened for easy viewing of the TV-type monitor by the radiology tech.

Four forty-five was my usual time to arise on workdays and it felt good to be lying down. After about ten minutes I turned to look at the screen. I'm always interested in learning new things and certainly fascinated with seeing parts of my own body that can't otherwise be seen.

"Tell me what you're seeing," I said.

"This is the portal artery," she said. That's the main artery in the liver.

Well, that's easy enough, I thought. I could see that it was pulsating.

"This is the portal vein. The circulation looks good," she went on.

OK so far. On the screen I could see a rather large area that looked white. It was odd in shape like a large wad of white gum smeared both directions on the sidewalk from someone's shoe, if it were possible to do that. Or maybe a picture from a Rorschach test. She moved the probe away from it then back several times, taking pictures. There was some discomfort with the movement of the probe but it was not unbearable.

"What's that white area?" I asked.

Suddenly the free flow of information stopped, but the tone of her voice was unchanged.

15

"Oh, I couldn't tell you about your test."

I recognized the words as though they were lines in a play I'd seen a hundred times. It was the kind of reply a nurse might give if she had information about a patient that had not yet been disclosed to him by his physician. Techs, like nurses, are not licensed to diagnose.

This can't be good, I thought. We were both silent as she finished the exam. Though I was sure she had some idea of what she was seeing, I did not press for more information. When she had finished the exam, the next ominous statement was pronounced.

"I'm going to run this by the radiologist. Wait here and I'll be back in a few minutes." Not, 'Go ahead and get dressed and your doctor will call you with the results.' Those few minutes seemed like an hour. Already the twenty-minute exam had taken nearly forty minutes and my work was waiting for me. I felt torn between the rising fear about what as wrong and the need to return to my job.

The tech returned. "The radiologist saw something he feels should be investigated further. He's calling your family doctor now. They'll be in touch with you later today."

I could sense a growing loss of control over the situation. It was more than a little unsettling.

"May I have breakfast now?" I am subject to migraines and was sure one would set in if I had to wait much longer for food.

"No, I'd wait until your doctor calls." She said.

This was getting ugly. And so do I when I can't eat!

"It Looks Like Liver Mets"

Having returned to my desk I shared what little I knew with my workmate, Susie. In the past year her husband had undergone treatment for cancer and she had shared some of his experience with me. I knew that he was doing well under the care of Dr. Powell, a local oncologist. I tried to dismiss a growing dread that I might need his services.

Soon the phone rang at my desk. It was Dr. Neidhardt. He spoke deliberately.

"There are some spots in your liver, Cheryl. It looks like liver mets." There was more information but the impact of those words was so profound the rest was lost. "Mets" is medical shorthand for metastasis. No easing into this possible diagnosis. Just …it looks like liver mets. Translation: you have cancer. And not just cancer in your liver but it didn't start there. It has come from somewhere else.

"I've talked to the radiologist," he went on as my thoughts returned to the immediate conversation, "and we feel it would be wise to do a CT scan… today at 2:30… might need a colonoscopy, … so don't eat or drink anything."

What does one do with this news? How do you wrap your brain around those words? How could the radiologist be sure? The impact of this discussion was difficult to process. The nurse in me took over. He said *colonoscopy*.

"If I need a GI doc, I want Dr. Sheikh," (pronounced 'shake') I said.

His voice still calm, he replied, "OK. I'll give him a call just to give him a heads-up, and we'll see what the scan shows." I was still on the clock.

I Need My Husband!

At this point I had not yet talked with Earl, my lifelong friend and soul mate, my husband of 38 years. We had been born the same year, only five days apart, living only half a block apart. We have literally known one another all our lives.

Married at the age of 21 while I was still a student nurse, we had four children who were by this time all married. They had produced four unbelievably beautiful and smart grandchildren, two boys and two girls whom we adore. We are in a constant state of amazement at the things they do and say. (And before this time we thought it was their *parents* who were so adorable and smart!)

Today I knew Earl was at home sleeping. He and our 26-year old son had been substituting on an early morning newspaper route and this was the last day. My husband, who was retired, went along more for the camaraderie than anything else. It gave him and Mark some time alone together that they both enjoyed. He had been up until about 5 A.M. and needed some sleep.

But I needed him now. He knew about the ultrasound, of course, so when I woke him from sleep I tried to relate the news gently.

Though he sometimes has a gruff exterior, he is really quite sensitive. In case this turned out *not* to be what it appeared I did not want to cause undue alarm.

"You'll need to come to the hospital about 2 o'clock today so you can be with me for a CT scan this afternoon. They've found some spots in my liver that they want to examine more closely. It could be bad, but we'll see." He would, of course, be there in time for the exam.

I tried to work but found it difficult to concentrate. There was this unknown "thing" going on in my body that now had taken over my thoughts.

"I Want to Do What Ever I Can to Help You"

The phone on my desk rang again. Grateful for something to do to occupy my mind, I picked it up. This time it was Dr. Sheikh. I had not expected him to call.

"I have spoken with Dr. Neidhardt," he said. "Cheryl, I want to do whatever I can to help you. You just tell me what it is that you need. If you need a procedure I will get you on the schedule as soon as possible. It doesn't matter what my schedule is, I will get you on in a day or two." Surprised by the call, I muttered my appreciation.

This was more than I could have expected from a man for whom I have the greatest respect as a physician. I had worked alongside him for more than two years, having gone to the endoscopy department just a few months before he came to our community to practice. So, I was still new to the work when he arrived and he had demonstrated remarkable patience with me. As it turns out, he treats everyone that way. He is in every sense of the word a gentleman.

Over the next two and a half years I learned a lot about endoscopic procedures and took my turn being on call regularly. I knew that emergency procedures, such as active bleeding situations, could be done within hours. Urgent work could be scheduled in a week or two, while routine procedures might be scheduled a month or two out. I would wait for his call after the CT scan had been read.

By 5:30 that day the scan was finished and we were on our way home. I still had not eaten and the migraine had made its appearance. I medicated the headache, ate dinner and collapsed into bed.

A Marathon

On Thursday I got up at 4:45 as usual, showered, dressed, had breakfast, and took my usual route to work. Everything in the office was the same as usual. How could this be an ordinary day when the possibility of cancer loomed so heavily on my horizon? Another co-worker Ruth, who was there that day, talked calmly with me off and on throughout the day.

"There are so many things it could be... I know it's hard to wait for the CT results... Dr. Sheikh is really good..."

They were words of reassurance I had spoken to others in similar situations. Only now I was on the receiving end. I couldn't concentrate on my work. It was all I could do to get the numbers in proper order to operate the FAX machine. It was hard for me to put two good thoughts back to back. Ruth's gentle kindness was so welcome that day.

Then the call came. The CT scan had confirmed the ultrasound. It was metastatic disease. Later I read the printed report in the computer, so clear in black and white. It seemed surreal to see this one with my own name on it, my date of birth. I had seen similar reports before, but they always applied to someone else. It was someone else's grief over the dreaded disease that everyone fears. I was always the one standing beside the bed, straightening the covers, offering comfort, busy starting the IV that would carry the medicine of hope, holding the hands and sometimes weeping.

The report read: "Innumerable coalescing hypodensities throughout the right and left lobes of the liver, highly suspicious for metastatic disease." Medical speak for lots of fused or growing together areas less dense than normal liver tissue. I would later learn that the actual involvement of the liver was about 90%. There were three large tumors, the largest being 7.4 cm in diameter (nearly 3") and smaller tumors scattered throughout the liver, so numerous they could not be counted. My worst fears had come true. The medical marathon had begun. I am not a runner but I was sure this event would be the most exhausting of my life.

Chapter 2

The Battery of Tests

In the ensuing hours there were more conversations with Dr. Neidhardt and Dr. Sheikh. I learned that the most common primary sites of cancer with lever metastasis are the colon, lung, and pancreas. I would need an upper scope exam (esophagogastroduodenoscopy, shortened to EGD for obvious reasons) to examine the esophagus and stomach, as well as a colonoscopy to look for tumors in the colon.

True to his word Dr. Sheikh scheduled the EGD for Friday, the *next day*. The colonoscopy was scheduled for Saturday. This truly impressed me as Saturday was reserved only for emergency procedures and this was *not* Dr. Sheikh's weekend to be on call. He was willing to come to work on his weekend off just for me!

EGD

The following day I presented myself in my old workplace department for the EGD. Several of my former workmates appeared in the room and greeted me with strained looks and warm hugs. Pat, Barb, Lisa, Donna, and Kathy were there. It was comforting to see familiar faces. But they had seen the diagnosis and knew its implications. The words unsaid spoke volumes.

It seemed odd to be on one of the carts that I had stood beside countless times. But my friends were there and I was pretty much at ease, though I'm sure Earl was not. But, as I had done with him during the phone call the previous Thursday, he hid his emotions from me.

Intravenous medication is administered during these procedures that renders the patient sleepy yet able to respond to commands, such as, "Turn on your side." Most people don't remember anything about the procedure due to the sedation. However, some patients are a bit difficult to manage or restless, through no fault of their own, and I did not want to be a problem patient.

To my relief, the sedation worked well and everything went smoothly. There was inflammation in the esophagus and stomach, but no mass or lesion was identified.

Upon learning that I was taking an anti-inflammatory drug for arthritis, which thins the blood slightly, Dr. Sheikh decided to delay the colon procedure until the following Tuesday. That would allow time for the medicine to get out of my system and, he said, "If there are polyps or, God forbid, a tumor, I would want to take care of it immediately." Being off the arthritis medicine for several days would reduce the chance of bleeding heavily if it became necessary to remove polyps or a tumor.

I called in sick that weekend. There was no use trying to work while existing on a clear liquid diet in preparation for the colonoscopy, and by now my nerves were very much on edge. I did not know then that I would never return to work.

Colonoscopy

By the morning of the procedure my aching joints confirmed that the arthritis drug was out of my system. Two small polyps were removed that morning and sent to the pathology lab, and some small outpouchings (diverticula) in the colon were identified. But there was no inflammation present.

I'd had every intention of watching the goings-on on the monitor, due again to that curiosity with seeing inner parts of my own body. But the IV drugs prevailed over my desire to see the inside of my colon. The sleep was wonderful and I remember nothing of the procedure or the day.

Dr. Sheikh had scheduled a liver biopsy for 7:30 the next morning and an MRI of the pancreas for Friday. I would also have an office visit with him late that afternoon. It would be then that I would be told the results of the tests.

The marathon was under way and I felt as though I had been pulled from the sidelines to compete unprepared.

Liver Biopsy

My recollection of this procedure is that one should never volunteer for it if you don't need it! Though the staff members made every effort to make me as comfortable as possible, it was definitely not comfortable. I was positioned on my back on the scanner bed, arms above my head. This is done to expand the rib cage as much as possible, lifting it away from the liver and other abdominal organs.

An instrument (I believe it is called a cannula) was placed just below the ribs and into the liver. Placement was checked using the CT scanner. Following a minor adjustment in placement, the biopsies were obtained. During each scan and biopsy I was told to carefully control my breathing, trying to breathe in and out the same amount each time. This is done so as not to damage surrounding organs. Try that with your arms over your head. It's hard. It felt as though someone had stabbed me and left the knife in place. Essentially, that's what it was.

MRI

The MRI was next on the menu of tests. I was now seeing firsthand more of the radiology department and its expensive equipment than I ever wanted to see. The MRI was very confining and I was relieved to have a washcloth placed over my eyes, keeping that confinement from my visual awareness. I have mild claustrophobia and though I had been given an anti-anxiety drug, I did not feel its effect. I could feel the sides of the "tube" against my arms as the machine moved me slowly through the narrow channel, taking its magnetic images. It made a loud "hammering" sound off and on during the 45-minute test.

I had been invited to bring a CD from home if I wanted to listen to music during the exam and I had brought one with music from the Kingdom Hall, our place of worship. This particular CD is an orchestral arrangement, and as I listened to the beautiful music the words to the songs ran through my mind.

"HAND IN HAND WITH GOD JEHOVAH,
WE WOULD HUMBLY WALK EACH DAY.
O HOW UNDESERVED THIS KINDNESS
THAT HE GRANTS TO MEN OF CLAY..."

And later:

"GIVE PRAISE TO JEHOVAH, BY HIS LOVE DIVINE.
YOU HAVE THIS COMMISSION HIS TRUTH TO LET SHINE.
YOU HAVE NOTHING WORTHWHILE YOU DID NOT
RECEIVE
FROM GOD YOUR PROVIDER, TO HIM HONOR GIVE...."

There was more, of course, but those are the ones I remember. It was so peaceful. The exam was over before I had heard the entire CD.

From My Journal:
This is shaping up to be a possibly all-encompassing, life-changing event. What will we find?

Chapter 3

"I've Been Thinking
How to Tell You..."

Now all that remained on this twentieth day of February was the visit with Dr. Sheikh. We arrived in the waiting room early. I filled out the usual paper work and was shown to an exam room by his young office assistant. I was sure she was younger than my children. She gave me a big smile as she directed us to the room. Did that mean the news was good? Surely she knew what the news was. Would she smile like that if it were really bad? Because that would give me false hope. What did it mean?

We waited in the smaller than usual room. I sat on the exam table. Earl was in the only chair. Thoughts of what might occur here came and went. Though I tried not to "buy" trouble mentally, the unthinkable was lurking in the background. Preferring not to consider the probability of cancer, I distracted myself with examining my surroundings.

Waiting to See the Doctor

There was the customary stool with wheels for Dr. Sheikh. On the back of the door there was a chart. It was a view of the entire human digestive system from mouth to rectum as though the body had been sliced in two from head to rump and upper thighs. I had seen a similar chart hundreds of times when I worked in Endoscopy. But to pass the time I looked at it again as though it were new to me.

I remembered countless visits to other doctors, mostly the pediatrician. Being the mother of four children those visits were frequent for many years. It was on those visits that I encountered difficulties, usually with my beloved only son, Mark. He had a curiosity that was boundless, so while I was busy with one or more of his sisters, he would be exploring every nook and cranny of the room.

24

What was in this drawer? Could he write on that paper? What did this thing on the wall do? How could he turn the light on? Could he have one of the latex gloves? How much did he weigh today? It was easier if he were the one who was ill. Then the only challenge was keeping him on the table while waiting for the doctor to arrive.

Once when his next older sister was being examined, the doctor lifted the top of her jeans and panties to palpate her abdomen. *This* was something Mark had never seen! He was pretty sure it wasn't right and demanded, "Get your hand out of my sister's pants!" She was mortified, and I think that was the last time he went to the doctor with us when she was ill!

Once in his pre-teen years, Mark entertained himself by blowing up an examining glove like a balloon while waiting for the doctor to arrive. He found this to be quite amusing. It must have tickled me that day which no doubt gave impetus to his further balloon-making antics whenever we visited a doctor's office or someone in the hospital.

Accompanying his father to far fewer doctor's visits, (Who can get a man to *go* to the doctor anyway?) it became clear to me from where this penchant for investigating medical exam rooms had come. I always feared the doctor would enter the room while some forbidden item from a drawer was being handled!

However, on this day my husband behaved himself. Neither of us could find much to be amused with on this Friday afternoon. So we waited in deafening silence. I sat on the table, swinging my feet forward and back, bored with the chart on the door.

"You Have Adenocarcinoma..."

After what seemed like an eternity but was actually less than ten minutes, Dr. Sheikh entered the room.

He is a tall, slender man, well over six feet tall with thick black hair. His original home was in Pakistan. Although his English is flawless, he has just enough of an accent that one knows he once spoke another language fluently. His expression is kind, but today he appears uneasy and his thick black brow is knit. He remains standing and begins to speak almost before the door is closed. I remember him practically pacing the floor in the tiny space available for his lanky frame.

"I've been thinking how to tell you and I think it is better to just be direct." He stopped pacing. "Cheryl, you have Adenocarcinoma of the liver." Now the recollection of the smile on the face of his office assistant seemed hollow and meaningless.

How typical of Dr. Sheikh to labor over *how* to give me this news! I had always recognized a keen sensitivity in this man for his patients' feelings and needs and now it was being demonstrated in my behalf.

My immediate reaction was almost no reaction at all. Though I cannot say I was surprised, I was deeply disappointed. I felt so vulnerable. And of course, there were those images in my mind of former cancer patients I had seen in my years as a nurse.

Dr. Sheikh talked on and through the medical jargon that was all too familiar to me, the realization that Adenocarcinoma meant cancer swept over Earl's face. Immediately his face reddened and there were tears.

I got off the exam table to comfort him and tried to listen to this man who this day seemed more like a friend. Dr. Sheikh continued. "Cancer is very treatable today... You're strong and otherwise healthy, and we can use very aggressive treatments... What oncologist would you like to see?"

It was impossible to dismiss the thought any longer. Thankful for my close working relationship with Susie and knowing about her husband's experience, I knew what my choice would be.

"I want Dr. Powell." I said.

He left us alone for several minutes while the appointment was made. We cried briefly together and attempted to compose ourselves.

I would see my oncologist on Monday for the first time, only three days away. For now, this man with whom I had so much enjoyed working was pulling out all the stops. He moved matters quickly, getting me on the schedule for a procedure within 24 hours, and now scheduling an appointment with the oncologist within the same time frame, excluding the weekend.

As we were leaving, Dr. Sheikh put his arm around my shoulders and gave me a hug. I could see the concern in his eyes and hear it in the tone of his voice. This man genuinely cares for me as a person, I thought. I had definitely made the right choice.

There's No Mistake

What lay ahead as we went home was to tell our four children what we had learned. This would be more difficult for us than getting the news ourselves. Angie, Mark and Sarah lived in Lima and our second daughter Christy, lived and worked in Columbus, along with her husband Darrin and daughter Megan. We worried about her making the two-hour trip to Lima, knowing that something was terribly wrong. So we dispatched Angie's husband, Steve, with Sarah and Tony to bring her. For now, only Christy would be coming to town.

We were glad that Mark had moved his family to Lima just three years previously. He and Natalie had lived in Tiffin since their marriage in 1997 and Mark was employed at a factory there. It paid well, but the job took a physical and spiritual toll on him. So he had decided to come back to Lima and look for work here. We opened our home to them and little Hannah who was about 15 months old at the time. It had been fun having a little one in the house again.

Two weeks after they moved here a tornado hit the apartment complex where they had lived, ripping the roof off of one of the three-story buildings and disrupting many lives. The timing of Mark's move had proved to be fortuitous.

Is This a Death Sentence?

By the time the group arrived from Columbus, everyone else had gathered at our home. We wanted to give this information to all of them at once.

We broke the news much the way Dr. Sheikh had done. The children were aware that I had been having some tests done. I explained that all the tests showed cancer. Metastatic disease, although the primary source was still unknown. Having grown up with a nurse in the house they all understood the gravity of the situation.

There were sobs of frustration and fear. Angie was sure she could donate part of her liver. We are so much alike she was positive it would be a perfect match. Were the doctors absolutely sure of the diagnosis, Mark wanted to know? Christy inquired if perhaps there was some mistake? Could there be some other cause for what they were seeing in the liver? Sarah, the youngest, could not find words through her tears.

No, they were sure. The biopsy had eliminated any doubt. None of us said it aloud but we were all thinking the same thing…

This is a death sentence.

Ninety percent of the liver was involved and that's only the area to which the cancer has spread! How bad must it be in the primary site? There were many questions and at this point, very few answers.

How Do I Tell Mom?

What remained was to inform my mother who was living in Florida. How do you tell your mother that you have cancer? Do you tell her how advanced it is? That you might not survive? This would be very difficult as I could not be there to comfort her or see her reaction. Getting this sort of news is bad enough. Getting it over the phone seemed worse.

I knew she was very close to her neighbor, Dorothy. She had previously given me her friend's phone number, so I called Dorothy first to be sure she was at home. I told her that I had some bad news to tell Mom and that she would need some comforting after our conversation. This brought some peace to my mind that at least Mom would not be alone for a while after hearing this news.

It would be much later that I would learn how truly heartbroken she was that day and continued to be throughout my treatment. She wished she could trade places with me. I, on the other hand, felt relieved that it was *not* one of the people I love so dearly who was ill. It's easier to be sick myself.

That weekend was Sarah's first wedding anniversary. The entire family gathered together. Christy's husband and daughter had arrived on Saturday and they all came for a meal at our house on Sunday. We took lots of pictures of me with all my kids.

How many more gatherings like this would we have? There was no way to know. This was our weekend of mourning together.

Clockwise from back left; Mark, me,
Angie, Sarah, and Christy.
Feb. 22, 2004

Seemingly, Mark was hit the hardest with this news but he wouldn't allow his anguish to last long. He would prove to be the one who changed our attitude toward this intrusion into our lives. He simply got up one day several weeks later and told himself it was of no benefit to continue to mourn. There was work to be done. He looked at this as a challenge and helped the rest of us to see it that way, too. We would not wallow in our sorrow. Though the odds were not in favor of recovery, that was our hope. If not recovery, then death with dignity.

Meeting My Oncologist

The waiting room was large with two rows of chairs back to back in the middle and several more lined up along the walls. Two large Thomas Kinkade paintings and a woven throw adorned the walls. There were lighthouses everywhere, symbols of hope. This is the Hope Center for Cancer Treatment. I liked it. I would learn in later conversations with Dr. Powell that his wife was a breast cancer survivor and it was she who had chosen the name for the center.

There must have been other patients waiting that day but I don't remember them. I signed the clipboard. *Cheryl Fisher.* The nurse was now officially the patient, waiting to see her cancer specialist. I was assembling my medical team and Dr. Powell would be at the helm.

As we were led through the door to the examining rooms we passed what appeared to be a ship's bell hanging on the inside wall by the door. A plaque hung just above it. We did not need to read it today, however. An article about that bell had appeared in a recent copy of our local newspaper.

One of the Hope Center's patients had decided that there should be some way of celebrating when each patient finished his chemotherapy. So the bell was purchased, mounted on a beautiful walnut plaque, and placed by the door. After the receiving the last dose of chemo, each patient may ring that bell with all his or her might! There was a goal to reach!

All four of the children wanted to be present for this meeting with Dr. Powell and hear with their own ears what to expect. How could I choose who would come and who would not? So there we were, all six of us in a room only slightly larger than our bathroom.

The nurse brought extra chairs and still some of them stood. I don't know who sat and who stood. All I remember is that my place was on that table.

What's He Like?

Dr. Powell is perhaps 5 feet 8 or so with light brown hair. He is wearing a dress shirt and tie and the traditional mid-thigh length, white medical jacket. His name is embroidered neatly over the left chest pocket. His appearance is very professional.

Dr. David Powell. D.O.

He seems to be surprised by the crowd of people in his exam room. His expression is kind, and I like him immediately. That is critical since I would be literally putting my life in his hands.

We reviewed my medical history and everyone but Earl was ushered out while Dr. Powell performed the physical exam. He had the previous test results. Nothing conclusive could be determined so we would continue to search for the primary site of the cancer. Blood was drawn and sent off for testing.

He spoke with confidence, giving us some information about treatment options once we knew what we were dealing with, and we left that meeting feeling somewhat better. At last someone was in charge of this situation.

We have never been told that it was due to this meeting, but several weeks later we noticed signs on the inside of the exam room doors that read, "DUE TO THE SIZE OF THE EXAM ROOMS, ONLY TWO PERSONS MAY ACCOMPANY THE PATIENT DURING VISITS WITH THE DOCTOR." Hmmm. Was our family the reason for these notices? We never asked.

From My Journal:
The schedule of go here, do this, let them do that, take this, etc. has been very hectic. Then there is this incredible, bone-tired feeling, partly due to the Percocet from Dr. Powell, which at least allows me to function at some level, free of pain.

This is all so confusing. I wonder how much time I have?

Chapter 4

"I Might as Well Get My Mammogram Done"

Being accustomed to taking care of my own health I thought I would schedule a mammogram while I was off work. It had been due in November, but I had postponed it due to a fall vacation and the early months of preparation for the "Magnet" thing at work. It was to be done on February 25th. It all seemed routine and I felt good about getting it done during some "down" time. Little did I know that I had probably just stepped ahead of Dr. Powell.

"I Would Say Leave it Alone"

Being a proponent of preventive health, I'd had mammograms done regularly for the past seventeen years. Not every year, because the reports always came back OK. During that time we'd had four different family doctors. (One retired, one moved out of town, and visits to a third one became inconvenient because of his location.)

Twice during this time there had been mention of a "lump" or "nodule" in the right breast, although it was not brought to my attention until the **second** time it was seen. Because I had not been told it was there I had waited five years to get the second mammogram! (What <u>nurse</u> would do that? I never have figured out how that fell through the cracks.) I consulted a local surgeon for a second opinion as soon as I was aware of the lump.

He had said, "Lumps are either benign or malignant. They don't change from one to the other. Given the location of this lump and the fact that it has not changed in five years, I would say it isn't going to change. If you were my wife, I would say 'Leave it alone.'"

At the time it seemed like a pretty good recommendation. It gave me some peace of mind. It was what every woman wants to hear.

I always mentioned this lump to the mammogram technician. Subsequent tests had not shown it again and the notes from the doctor always read, "No change from previous exam," or "Your mammogram was OK."

Of course, I never saw the formal reports that said, "A negative mammogram should not deter the workup of a clinically suspicious lesion." And, "There are densities in both breasts that could obscure a lesion." That information was on the official report sent to the doctor.

I saw what Angie refers to as the "feel-good" note from the doctor's office, pre-printed and signed by the doctor. No room for something *clinically suspicious,* only two choices. It was either OK or not OK. I always got the OK letter, so I occasionally went every *other* year for mammograms. After all, the nodule was never palpated on exam, either by my doctors or during self-exams.

Two years previous to the current event, I had mentioned to my gynecologist and to the mammogram tech that I had noticed something unusual about my right breast. When I would raise my arm, during bathing or putting on deodorant, the right nipple would "blanch" or lose all its color and appear very pale. Neither of those professionals asked to observe that, and neither seemed concerned by this phenomenon. I concluded it was just an oddity in my breast.

Now what had always seemed routine became anything but that.

One of These Things is NOT Like the Other

The mammogram films were done on Wednesday, February 25, 2004. A call came from the Women's Health Center the following day. The radiologist had seen some "densities" on the films that she wanted to examine more closely. Could I come in Friday for more films?

The additional mammogram films were done using a smaller plate with which to "crush" my breast. I was told that this allowed a more precise film to be obtained since they were now looking at a specific location and not the entire breast.

A doctor there in the Women's Health Center examined the films. Before I could be invited to get dressed the tech informed me that the doctor had suggested having a right breast ultrasound done. That exam could be done immediately. When it was completed the doctor recommended an ultrasound-guided needle biopsy, which was also performed that same day. The offer was made to come back for these procedures in the next few days, but I was there and the equipment and personnel were available (I asked!) and I wanted it done *now*. Not tomorrow or next week!

Earl was in the waiting area during this time and no one thought to inform him about the extended proceedings until my suggestion to do so just before the biopsy. Having not accompanied me for previous mammograms, he had no idea how long it should take, but I knew he would soon tire of waiting and begin to worry.

We went home that afternoon anxious for our second meeting with my oncologist. These tests had taken more than two hours.

"You're It!"

The following Monday when I saw Dr. Powell again, we had our answers. I had reached what writer and cancer survivor Steven Roberts calls my "You're it" moment. The moment in which one is informed that *you* are the one person in eight in this country who has cancer. And, just as it is with the childhood game of "Tag," *no one* wants to be "It!"

Although intellectually I knew better, I had still harbored a small hope that somehow the final results would prove otherwise. The breast biopsy along with the results of blood tests (CEA, a broad range cancer indicator, and CA 27.29, the tumor marker for breast cancer) Dr. Powell had ordered had pinpointed the primary site of the cancer. I had *breast cancer!* Now we knew the origin of the cells that had already invaded my liver.

The location of this lump was *the same as the earlier mammograms!* It was at "11 o'clock," the upper outer quadrant of the right breast. Dr. Powell felt that this disease had been present for at least ten years, hidden inside my ample breast where it could not be detected easily, cells that *could* have been normal tissue densities but obviously were not.

I learned too late that just because a doctor tells you what you *want* to hear, that you may ignore something that has potentially bad consequences, it might not be true. Even if the recommendation comes from someone you know and trust, *get it checked out!* A competent physician will never deny nor be offended by the request for a second (or third!) opinion.

There was no history of cancer in our immediate family. No known reason for this dreaded disease to attack. I would later learn that up to 80% of breast cancers are detected in women with no family history of the disease.

Strangely enough, within eight months of my diagnosis, Earl's brother's wife called us from Florida where she had just been diagnosed with breast cancer. Norma's was Stage I and caught early enough that lumpectomy and radiation would be all the treatment she would need. However, her diagnosis meant that *all three* of the Fisher brothers' wives had had breast cancer! (The oldest brother's wife survived 15 years after her original diagnosis and lost her battle in 1998.) And of course, we were not otherwise related to one another. What bizarre circumstances!

The Race Strategy

Now what? Dr. Powell's plan of action was already in place. I would be given chemotherapy. We would start with Taxotere, a new generation of the highly successful breast cancer drug, Taxol. And, as Dr. Sheikh had predicted, it would be aggressive. I would have treatments every week for three weeks, then one week off. Then the cycle would start again.

Having worked for fourteen years as an IV Therapy nurse I did not want anyone, experienced or new, to be probing *my* arms week after week looking for not-so-prominent veins. I also knew that repeated puncturing of veins and chemotherapy damage the veins so that even good ones become more difficult to access over time. Thankful for this past nursing experience, and unsure of how many chemo treatments I would need, I requested a Medi-Port, a surgically implanted medical device for administration of IV medications. My appointment with the surgeon was the next morning.

Here is another instance where I feel so privileged to know the people that I do. Sharon, one of my closest friends, is also a nurse who works at another hospital in our community. She gave me the name of a surgeon, Dr. Sarah Olt, who has "a near zero percent" complication rate. Where else can one get that kind of information? So, of course Dr. Olt was my surgeon of choice. She scheduled the surgery for the coming Saturday, March 6. The procedure would be done in the morning using conscious sedation, like I'd had for the colonoscopy and EGD, and I would be home that afternoon.

Now that we knew what we were treating, there would be no further delay. That Tuesday afternoon, March 2, 2004 I was given my first dose of chemotherapy through a vein in my arm. A colleague and former workmate placed that IV catheter. It would be the only time I would receive chemo by that method.

A marathon runner would now be settling in to a steady pace. In this race, there would be no one to match pace with or pass. The goal was simply to finish.

You Have Breast Cancer in Your Liver!

One might ask, why don't they just yank that tumor out of there? That was certainly one of *my* questions.

The answer is that the disease in the liver was so advanced that the tumor in the breast was truly of little concern at that time. Dr. Powell's thoughtful, considerate answer was not, "It's really too late for that," but instead, "That might be unnecessary."

So there was brief talk of surgery later, most likely mastectomy. Though the prospect of losing a breast was horrific in itself, it sounded better than the alternative... loss of life altogether. So I began reading about mastectomy and how one heals, physically and emotionally, from this life-altering surgery.

Having not been an oncology nurse I had a lot to learn about this disease. I thought I had breast cancer *and* liver cancer. Nope! I had *breast cancer in my liver!*

To illustrate Dr. Powell's explanation of this, suppose you have a flower garden and a vegetable garden. If the wind blows some of the seeds from the flower garden into the vegetable garden, you don't have more vegetables just because the seeds landed there. You have *flowers in your vegetable garden!* So, the evil cells from the breast tumor went to the liver and I had *breast cancer in my liver!*

From my Journal:

Sarah washed my hair for me- again. That feels good.

Karen is coming to help with Mom's move. She says I can sit around and give orders.

Sarah and "Taylor-Tot" (her step daughter) *stayed after the meeting, as did Mark, Natalie and Hannah. The house was filled with little-girl voices and big-girl laughter! What fun!*

And the Race is On!

So, the treatment would be chemo. It would travel throughout my body in the bloodstream and attack the cancer cells wherever they might be.

Treatments number one and two went without a hitch, both given in the hospital where I worked, by nurses I knew and liked very much. They were more than kind to me and kept me informed of all the test results and blood work that had been done.

It seemed odd again to be *in* the bed on the oncology unit instead of running off to start someone's IV or answering call lights or reviewing charts. The transition from nurse to patient would not come easily.

My husband accompanied me to the chemo sessions, of course, as well as one or more of my children. My sister Ardy, whose husband had died from cancer the previous July, was there for the first treatment. It was too difficult for her to come after that. Wayne's death was so recent and it brought back painful memories that were more than she could endure on a frequent basis.

Sarah came with us for the second treatment, bringing a large bag along. Inside she had something she had been working on called a "knot" blanket. It is made of two layers of fleece knotted together on the edges. She finished it there in my room in time for me to cover up with it before the infusion was completed. It was warm and comforting, special to me since she had made it.

Ardy later made me a knot blanket too, with 'Breast Cancer Awareness' symbols all over it! I took one or the other of the two blankets to most of my treatments to keep me warm while the IV medication ran into my body, and I had Earl and my complement of children to keep me company.

From my Journal:

Sometimes it seems like this is all a ruse... a cruel joke. But because my medical regimen is so effective, I don't have-at least yet-all of the pain and nausea so often equated with this disease. Prevention of pain and nausea is easier than treatment! (I AM finding that I can't write, however. My hand doesn't always do what the brain tells it to do!)

I love it when the mail comes! I get cards EVERY DAY! And they outnumber the bills! ☺

The black-eyed susans broke ground in the front flowerbed!! Yea! Earl bought a grape vine for shade over the deck and my very own Stargazer Lilly bulbs - two of them! Spring is coming and so is Mom!

Stargazer lilies by the pond

My Black-eyed Susans

Almost Tripped

Trudging through three inches of fresh snow, I arrived for treatment number three. We were about halfway down the hall when a nurse confronted me and announced, "We tried to call but you had already left home!" The blood that was drawn the previous day showed the ANC (Absolute Neutrophil Count, a blood component that involves the white blood cells) to be too low to administer the chemo.

I was immediately so angry you would have thought she had accused me of a crime! I used to have a terrible temper that was displayed by slamming doors for the satisfyingly loud noise that was produced. I also used to stomp my feet, but stopped that when it began to make my legs hurt.

However, by this point in my life, having become a student of the Bible and learning that 'anger and wrath and abusive speech' (see the Bible book of Ephesians chapter 4, verse 31) are unacceptable in a true Christian's life, I had mostly gained control of my negative emotions. I say "mostly" because of human imperfection. The imperfection and old temper manifested itself now.

I stopped abruptly in my tracks and before I knew it I had again stomped my foot to the floor. I was clearly not in control of my emotions.

"NO!" I said. I was incensed and near tears instantly! I was beginning to feel the untoward effects of the chemotherapy and had just dragged myself out of bed and out into the snow only to hear that I had to go back home!

"I have a killer loose in my body. I've had two shots at it and you're telling me that I can't even load the gun this time?" I don't know from where the weapon analogy came. I'm not a proponent of violence and I've never even held a real gun in my hand! Perhaps I watch too many police shows on TV. But before I was even cognizant of the thought, those were the words that escaped my mouth.

When I regained my composure it was explained that if the ANC fell below 1.5 and the chemo was administered, my entire immune system would be defenseless. A common cold or other minor infection could lead to my death. My ANC was 1.4. Now, *that* made sense to me.

I apologized for my behavior and went home. My body must have got the message that I did not want to delay treatments because *never* after that did the ANC fall too low to receive the chemo!

From my Journal: *I am thankful that:*
In general, I feel better than I could have ever
believed with cancer. (Can't help but
wonder...when will it get worse?)

   -I have been able to tie my own shoes again for several days now.
(Previously my feet were too swollen and it was painful to bend
over.)
   -I can wash my own hair.
   -I choose NOT to wear make-up unless I really want to.
   -I have pain, but it is controlled.
   -I am tired and that's OK.
   -MOST DAYS ARE GOOD.
   -ALL DAYS HAVE SOME HAPPINESS!

Chapter 5

Mother

Back in the fall of 2003 I'd had a phone conversation with my mother, Bernice LaViness, (pronounced luh-VYE-ness) who was living in Port Charlotte, Florida. She had moved there a year or so following my father's death in 1983, something they had planned to do together. It had been a difficult adjustment, eased somewhat by the fact that two of her siblings and their mates had been living there for many years already. There were less than forty miles or so separating the three of them, and her sister Thelma was only a few miles away.

The two girls had bonded together early in life when their mother died at the age of 26. The girls were only eight and ten at the time. They had always been close and this sad time had cemented their relationship. But at such a tender age, they were separated from their father and three brothers and raised by their grandmother. Life was not easy, but they grew to be successful in their chosen careers, Mom as a bank vice president and Thelma as a nurse.

In their retirement years they had grown very close again but by now both her brother and sister had died. Mom was without family in Florida and had only a few close friends that she had met when she moved to her present location. Visits from my sisters and me were infrequent due to our busy families and work.

During this particular conversation Mother surprised me by saying that she was planning to move back to Ohio! I knew that she had been diagnosed with macular degeneration, a condition that would rob her of her eyesight over time. Though she had received some treatments designed to arrest the disease, there is no cure for it. She knew she would eventually need to be near her children for support and possible assistance in the future. She felt it was better to make the move while she could still see fairly well. She wanted to live in Lima.

Cheryl's family; standing, from left, Ardy Fark, Karen Norris, and Cheryl. Seated is their mother, Bernice LaViness. This photo was taken in 2003.

Finding a New Home for Mom

We talked about how to make this move a smooth one. Mom had asked us to look at possible homes for her here. During November and December we toured about ten different places, discussed them over the phone and sent her photos of the most likely prospects. It seemed like an unusual way to purchase a home, but what else could be done from this distance?

Mom said, "If you like it I know I will."

The condo she chose was newly constructed and very attractive, only a few miles from our home. I had busied myself early that winter on my days off scheduling the things she could not take care of from 1,100 miles away.

By the time my diagnosis was made plans were well under way for her move. She would be ready to come here by the end of March.

It distressed me that I could not be in Florida to assist with the packing, but my sister Ardy had gone down for the month of January and much of the packing had been accomplished then. Her plans were beginning to come together and soon she would be closer to all of us.

Just in Time!

The timing of Mom's move turned out to be better than we could have imagined. The year 2004 was a near record-breaking year for hurricanes in and around the Gulf of Mexico and the west coast of Florida.

In the 21 years Mom had lived there, no hurricane had hit the area where she lived. However, within months after she came to Ohio, two hurricanes went right through Port Charlotte and the condo complex where she had lived was hit both times! There was extensive damage in the area and what was left of the complex had become uninhabitable due to the growth of mold. Had she stayed there, not only would she have been forced to move, but we would have been unable to help her. And her property would have been worthless!

From my journal:
Things to ponder over:
-I still have my hair!
-I like my new "Scooby-Do" toothbrush!
*   (see Helpful Hints)*
- Temps are rising outside- 36 degrees this a.m.

The Moving Van Arrives

Earl and Steve, with their road-weary passenger, made the trip home as planned and there was a tearful reunion with Mom. I'm sure she felt somewhat better about my illness after seeing that I was doing reasonably well, and I certainly felt better having her here. It seems, no matter how old I get, there are just times when I feel better having my mother close. This was one of those times.

We had recently redecorated our guest room and hoped she would be comfortable there temporarily. It would be several days before the moving van was to arrive with her furniture.

There had been a technical delay in Mom's receiving the funds from the sale of her condo. This caused her no small amount of anxiety. This money represented nearly her entire life savings, and she had been forced to leave the state without having the check from the real estate agent in her possession.

The details were worked out and it was promised that the money would be deposited to her account in Ohio by April 2. The closing on her condo here was scheduled for the same day. The two transactions were scheduled only hours apart and we were hoping for a smooth progression of events.

It was finally accomplished with only a couple of hiccoughs! Her bank called to inform us that the deposit had been made, and the papers were signed at the builder's office within the hour. All that remained was for her furniture to arrive.

The moving van was due in Lima on Monday. The driver had given Mom his cell phone number, and a call to him brought the unhappy news that he was still in Florida on Monday! In the end, he did not arrive until Wednesday, a delay which caused my poor mother more unnecessary anxiety.

But finally, it was done. She was in her own place and spring was on its way. It was still much colder here than she had been used to in Florida for the past 21 years, but she was here. And for the mother and sick daughter, that was all that mattered.

From my Journal:

The cardinals are up early and singing in the back yard. The sky is overcast and starting to drip a little, but the temperature is approaching 60 degrees already. It looks like we have beaten winter out one more time!

I am thankful for:
-Short-term disability!
-My husband who loves my family so much and takes good care of my mother.
-My sisters. Having Ardy here this week was great and Karen is coming next week to help settle Mom in. It will be like having an extended "sleep-over!"

Girls' Night Out!

At the end of March our local Symphony Orchestra was presenting a concert that included some Gershwin music. The first biography I ever read was about George Gershwin. I was about ten at the time and reading someone's life story was fascinating to me. Over the years I had grown to love the music he and his brother Ira had produced. Later I had been active in vocal music in school, and took piano lessons for a short time. I still love music.

Lima has had a symphony orchestra for 50 years, but I had never been to a concert. Knowing there would be a tribute to Gershwin, I did not want to miss this one! It was scheduled for the last Saturday in March.

From my Journal:

Today I am thankful that:

- *I am currently at all of the meetings at the Kingdom Hall.*

-I get to have chemo again tomorrow.

-Earl is WONDERFUL!

-Chives are growing by the pond.

-I have four wonderful children and four beautiful grandchildren!

Dangerous Crowds

Since I would have had to miss at least one dose of chemo to go along on the trip to get Mom, Earl and I felt it was best for me to stay in Ohio. So Angie's husband Steve went along. This left me free for chemo and the Symphony, if Dr. Powell would approve. Knowing it was important to watch for low blood counts and to exercise caution in large crowds due to the danger of infections, I asked Dr. Powell's permission to attend the proceedings. So, it was with his blessing that I got tickets to the Gershwin concert and made plans to attend.

My widowed sister Ardy had also taken piano lessons, much longer than I had, and I invited her to go with me. I anticipated a wonderful evening for both of us. Besides everything else, I wanted to do as much as I could in whatever time I had left.

We decided to dress up for this event, and have dinner at a local downtown restaurant before the concert. It would be a spectacular 'Girls' Night Out!'

From my Journal:

I am thankful for:
- Being surrounded by good family and friends. All of the Utilization Staff went to dinner with me tonight at Milano Grill! Susie, Ruth, Kathy, Laura, Cindy, Terry, and Shirley.
-I am still mobile.
-Sarah, who does my nails every week!
-Prayer that is a powerful tool.

Hair Today, Gone Tomorrow!

Saturday morning dawned with gray skies, but worse things were happening inside. I knew that alopecia, or total hair loss, is common during chemotherapy and had looked at a catalog of hats and wigs. Because there seemed to be no dramatic change in my hair, I had delayed placing an order. It proved to be a gross miscalculation on my part.

Several days before Earl and Steve left for Florida, I noticed a bit more hair on the floor of the shower each day. The Friday that they left, it was getting worse. By the morning of the concert, there were literally handfuls of hair on the shower mat, and even more underneath it. I had just sent the order for my hats the previous week and they were not here, but it was apparent that I *had* to have a hat for that night!

I went to a local store where they carry mastectomy supplies, lingerie, hats and other items for cancer patients. I found a hat that would go with my dress. It was $34, almost as much as I had paid for the five hats I had on order! But they weren't here, and I needed a hat. Besides, this was truly a special occasion.

The purchase was made and Ardy drove us home. Three hours later the mailman delivered my shipment of hats! I soothed my guilt over the pricey hat with the assurance that none of the hats in the shipment went as well with the dress.

Though the day had begun with clouds, by afternoon the sun was shining and the prospect of hearing some of my favorite music presented live was invigorating. All that remained before the big event was to get a nap and get dressed.

From my Journal:

Megan overheard her mom telling someone that my hair was coming out. Megan asked, "Did I hear you say Grammie's hair is coming out?" Christy said, "Yes, it's because of her medicine." Megan said, "I know how I'll recognize her even if she doesn't have any hair." Christy said, "How's that?" "By her eyes!"

Currently my goal is REMISSION. I feel very strongly that it is possible... I could be sicker. We'll see. I just want more time...

Picked up copies of every mammogram report I've ever had done from the hospital today. Why didn't I ask for the 'official' reports sooner? No reason to have done it, I guess.

I am thankful that bills are being paid by insurance.

We are Driven

Other than the usual tiredness from the chemo, alleviated somewhat by an afternoon nap, I felt almost as though we were kids again, getting ready for a big party! We even had a chauffeur!

Mark had agreed to drive us to dinner and then to the Civic Center for the concert. These two locations were really within walking distance of each other, but given my current circumstances, it would have been too much for me to do and still enjoy the evening. So we rode in the back seat of my PT Cruiser as though we were from another era, ladies of fashion with our own driver! He even got out and opened the doors for us! I think he enjoyed playing his role that evening.

Dinner was beautiful. Already food did not have much flavor for me but I enjoyed the colorful and artful appearance of it. I had eaten at this restaurant several times and had requested my favorite table by the window. There we could watch the sun sinking through the remaining clouds and enjoy the ambiance of the old brick-walled storefront restaurant.

The call to Mark was made after dinner and within minutes our driver delivered us to the Civic Center. Though I'd had no idea what seats to request when I had called for the tickets, I felt as though the ones we had were really special! They were in the middle of the concert hall only three rows back from the stage! The conductor wore a tuxedo, of course, and all the orchestra members were dressed in black suits or dresses. We were so close to the stage I had the feeling the maestro was talking just to my sister and me as he introduced each selection.

The first Gershwin piece was "An American in Paris." He introduced it well, helping us to imagine we were on the streets of Paris, hearing the cacophony of taxi horns and watching people as they hurried along.

Ardy and me, arriving for dinner the evening of the Lima Symphony Orchestra's concert featuring the music of George and Ira Gershwin.   Notice the "pricey" hat!

The conductor moved through the piece with precision, pointing his baton in the direction of each section in its turn. It was everything I had anticipated.

The highlight of the evening was the memorable "Rhapsody in Blue," my favorite piece played as I have never heard it before. The young piano soloist was spectacular. Playing this 20-minute piece with no sheet music before her, she presented an absolutely flawless performance! I was enthralled.

After the intermission there was a reading by a local artist of "The Road Not Taken" by Robert Frost, and a performance of Grofe's "Grand Canyon Suite." Though I have never seen the Grand Canyon, through the music I could envision a line of burros meandering up and down the canyon, carrying their burdens with sure-footed steps.

As we waited outside the concert hall for Mark to pick us up, the Spring air was fairly intoxicating. It was unseasonably warm for the end of March and though a light breeze was blowing we carried our coats. The music rang in our ears and our minds and we hummed the tunes on the ride home. Upon arriving, I put my Gershwin music in the CD player and we lounged away the remainder of the night, content with our musical memories.

From my Journal:

Ardy had roast pork and I had pecan-crusted chicken, mashed sweet potatoes and green and yellow wax beans with carrots. Couldn't eat it all so we sent it home with our good-looking driver!

I forgot to get the Gershwin music out this week to PREPARE for the evening, and during the pre-concert discussion they asked questions! I felt like I was back in school and hadn't done my homework!! Couldn't remember the names of the songs my favorite composers had written! Argh!

I am totally spent, but so happy!

I still have eyelashes!

Wearing my "Pretties"

Having been married for 38 years by this time and having a thoughtful husband, I have acquired a little nice jewelry. Nothing extravagant, you understand, just a few pieces that I like because they have family history or were gifts from Earl. I tend to be reasonably modest, not showy with them, so most of my jewelry remains in the armoire until special occasions. I would wear a piece to work occasionally, but the diamonds usually stayed at home except for my wedding rings and an anniversary ring.

Some weeks into treatment I fully understood that there really is no cure for my illness and that the most I could hope for was remission, and I thought to myself, "What am I saving these for? I might as well wear them!"

So on an occasion when all the children were home for a visit I wore my emerald earrings and necklace and a diamond tennis bracelet that was an anniversary gift. (Earl really is good, isn't he?) It must have seemed odd to Angie to see me wearing my special jewelry on a day at home when I was also wearing jeans. As we sat down to eat she commented on all of the "bling," as the kids refer to jewelry today.

I said, "Well, I figured I might as well wear my pretties while I can!" I hadn't intended to upset her by the comment, but to her it translated to, 'There may not be much time left to enjoy it.' She still tears up when she relates the story.

I continue to wear my "bling" on a daily basis. After all, I enjoy looking at it, too!

From my Journal:

Family news - Christy interviewed for and got a job HERE IN LIMA!! They wanted her so badly they offered her more than they had

advertised if she would accept the position! So they are trying to sell their house and have been looking at houses here. Darrin has been staying in Columbus with the dogs and Megan comes here with Christy every other week.

My dear son came over this evening and he has HAD HIS HEAD SHAVED! NOW WE ARE TWINS! What a demonstration of love!

Mark and Natalie will be having another baby in February!

Mark before he shaved his head.   **The two baldies!**

Chapter 8

The "Ballet" of Drugs

Now that mom was in town, she began accompanying us to many of the chemo sessions. She would call every Monday and ask who was planning to go along. If none of the children had "bid" on the spot, Mom would volunteer to be there. So we would pick her up on the way to the Hope Center. It became a regular Tuesday practice.

As spring approached that year I wondered if it would be my last. Through the haze of chemotherapy and pain medicine I tried to heighten my awareness of each blossom and leaf as they appeared.

I watched the birds at our feeders fluttering as they vied for a spot to perch for a few seconds and secure the precious bits of feed. I had observed this ritual for most of my life, as Dad has always fed birds and we had begun it soon after our marriage. It gave a sense of stability to life to see that these events- spring, migrating birds and new flowers- come reliably every year. I would enjoy whatever I could of these things for as long as I could. When I could summon the energy, I would take a walk through the yard, looking for each new plant and flower as it made its appearance out of its winter sleep.

From my Journal:
LET THE SHOPPING BEGIN! Karen and Ardy came today. Earl took us to Delphos to look at furniture for Mom's condo.
Found everything Mom needs but a small curio.

Cortisone

Patients on chemotherapy may be given some form (or several) of cortisone for its ability to counteract side effects of the chemo. It can prevent build-up of calcium in the blood and fight inflammation and allergic reactions. Those are its useful properties. This drug itself, however, has many complex reactions in the human body and can present its own set of side effects.

It produces a feeling of euphoria, insomnia, mood swings, increased blood sugar due to decreased ability to break down carbohydrates, swelling of extremities, muscle weakness, increased sweating, thin and fragile skin, and can cause the onset of Type II Diabetes. It did all of those things to me.

So eventually, to control the diabetes, two more drugs were added to my laundry list of medications and I began testing my blood glucose twice daily.

Cortisone can also allow dormant or latent infections to activate. The list of potential side effects of decadron is much longer. These are the ones I experienced. Others of note are impaired wound healing, masking of signs of infection, osteoporosis, headaches, and depression. As you can well imagine, it is not a drug to be treated lightly.

Some Side Effects May Occur...

Hours blended into days, days into weeks and weeks into months as I settled into a new routine. Start taking Decadron every Monday night about 9 PM, chemo every Tuesday for three weeks with the fourth Tuesday off. For most of that duration, including Tuesday and Wednesday nights I would get little sleep. Staying awake was not by choice, of course. The Decadron threw my body into overdrive and my brain would not shut down. I felt agitated and unable to sit or lie still much of the time. By Thursday I was more than tired, exhausted by Friday and Saturday.

Sundays I would drag myself out of bed, knowing that just to be able to see our friends at the Kingdom Hall, to be encouraged by them, to be able to worship our God Jehovah another day, all of that would make me stronger.

The morning shower was so tiring I needed to rest after getting dressed. So, we would go, and it was like being charged with energy while we were there. I would visit with our friends before the meeting began and for a few minutes afterward. It would be good to get back home again.

After a bite of lunch I would collapse, sometimes in bed, sometimes on the couch.

It would be there on the couch that I might drift in and out of "consciousness," but mostly unaware that anyone else in the world existed. The TV would be on, tuned very low. Off and on I would hear the mesmerizing up-and-down cheers of an NFL crowd or later the hum of NASCAR races or the crack of a bat as the Cleveland Indians tried one more time to make it to the post-season. There was also the familiar tune played during Chrysler commercials, new that first winter, which still reminds me of those somnolent days on the couch.

By most Mondays I would feel somewhat better. I might even do a load or two of laundry. But that night I would take the Decadron, and on Tuesday it would begin again. So it went throughout that late winter and the following summer.

I cherished my off weeks in the beginning, as I could begin to feel almost normal again. Later, the one week off was not enough to make much of a difference.

If It's On the List of Possible Side Effects, I Got It!

In addition to the typical "moon-face" of patients on heavy doses of steroids (I preferred to call it "chipmunk face.") the side effects to the Taxotere began to mount. Tears ran from my eyes almost constantly, and that to such an extent that I found it nearly impossible to read. This deprived me of one of my few remaining pleasures, as I have always been an avid reader.

Wearing makeup would only irritate my eyes more, and would have been wiped off soon with the tears anyway. I quit wearing it. Ask my children, previously I wouldn't dream of going out the door without full makeup and having shampooed my hair. Now I was too tired to care.

There was gradual deterioration of finger and toenails. This may seem minor when our nails are fully functioning, but it became really problematic over time. I could not scratch even a minor itch. I could not retrieve items from the floor if they were dropped, such as a coin, a paper clip, or a small piece of paper.

It became a challenge to separate pages in a book or plates on a shelf. It took concentration to prevent catching the jagged edges of the nails while folding clothes or even while showering and drying off. I began wearing socks to bed to prevent getting the toenails caught in the sheets. I limited the amount of time I had my hands in water, but that still did not prevent the onset of nail fungus. This led to visits to yet another specialist, one who treats infectious disease. It would be nearly two years before my nails would return to normal.

Nausea and occasional vomiting, complete hair loss, lethargy, numbness and tingling in fingers and toes, and fluid retention were also of concern. Most people might think of swelling in the ankles and legs as simply an annoyance. If it continues to progress, it can become life threatening.

Fluid builds up in the lower extremities and if left untreated, begins to back up into the lungs. Kidney function is affected due to fluid overload. In an attempt to prevent the swelling, I would sit with my feet elevated higher than my heart or level with my hips whenever possible.

Still, the fluid packed on. Some days my legs were so heavy with water I had to literally lift them with my hands to get into and out of the tub or the car. My weight might vary as much as eight to ten pounds over just a few days. It is exhausting to carry that much extra weight on an already overweight, exhausted body.

Another disconcerting effect of the chemo was that my nose ran almost continuously. Remember the numbness in my fingers and toes? Well, the tip of my nose was also numb, and I could not always feel it running until it would drip. So it was with love that my husband or one of my daughters would say, "You need a tissue."

There was also the problem of digestive disturbance. It fluctuated between constipation and diarrhea, and of course there was a need for the subsequent treatment for each of those conditions.

How Do You Counteract It?

The side effects were battled with an arsenal of- what else?- more drugs. A vitamin supplement to counteract the numbness and tingling, antinausea pills, another drug to keep me from sleeping round the clock, and a diuretic to rid my body of the excess water.

With all of this in addition to the pain medicine, I began to feel like a walking pharmacy.

After a few weeks on that regimen my blood pressure dropped dramatically and an adjustment had to be made in the blood pressure medicine as well. Everything seems to interact. One of my doctors refers to this as a "ballet" of medications. It is important to keep track of the performers in the ballet as they dance through the body.

I began keeping a chart of all the drugs, much as I had done when I was working at the hospital and giving medications to patients. I also made notes of my temperature and blood pressure, and "nurses notes" of a sort, recording new symptoms or persistent ones. It gave me something meaningful to do, even through the mental and physical exhaustion, and I had an accurate "report" for Dr. Powell on subsequent visits.

Is It Hot In Here? I Can't Sleep!

Perhaps the most socially disturbing of these side effects was the increased sweating, medically termed diaphoresis. It was worse than menopause had been! Sometimes two or three times during the day I would change all or most of my clothing because it was soaked with perspiration. It was really disturbing if I needed to be away from home. In public it is embarrassing to have perspiration pouring off of your head, making your hands, arms and legs clammy, and making your clothes cling to you.

Add to that the persistent insomnia. During the early therapy with Decadron I would sometimes go to bed late thinking surely then I would be able to sleep. Usually I could get two or three hours of good sleep. Then it seemed as though a switch had been flipped somewhere in my body. My eyes would pop open and suddenly all systems were on "Go!" It was as though my brain had been set on hyper mode. I could not stop the mental "wheels" from turning.

So at 2 or 3 AM I would get up and go to the kitchen. There I could turn lights on and read or make lists of things to do without disturbing Earl's sleep. Sometimes I would write in my journals. Other times I would indulge in scrapbooking, a hobby that brings me much pleasure. (More about that later.)

Chemo-Brain

There is a condition commonly found, particularly in women who are given chemotherapy. My girls think it sounds a bit degrading, but it is called chemo-brain. Thankfully, it is temporary, but it causes short-term memory loss.

Suddenly I could not remember what I was doing or why. Names escaped me. I could not remember the last time I took Percocet! I would go to some room in the house and not remember why I had gone there. This was not good at a time when mobility was impaired by so many drugs, making it difficult to navigate from one end of the house to the other.

It was very disturbing for this wife/mother/nurse who was used to being somewhat in control of her life to realize I was not even able to remember a simple computer password. Or whether or not I had fed the dogs.

I began keeping meticulous records of everything, fearing that I would forget something vital. More than once I even put some bills in a stack of papers intending to do something with them "later," then forgot where I put them. Then, there were times I wrote things down, and couldn't remember where I wrote them! Soon our home was plastered with "sticky" notes reminding me of appointments or medications or things to do.

In the end, Chemo-brain has become a good excuse for failing to remember certain things! I may be able to use this for quite a while. After all, who knows for sure how long it takes to rid your body of all those chemicals?

Chapter 9

Treatments at the Hope Center

After the first round of chemo, which consisted of the three doses with the one-week of interruption and the one off week, I decided to have the remainder of my treatments at the Hope center. Conversation with those I love helped to pass the time and there were television sets suspended from the ceiling above each patient chair. Sometimes we took the local newspaper along as a diversion, or a book to read. Later my mother gave me word or number puzzle books to work on. Those are very helpful in keeping the mind active.

I had just become used to the routine and more acquainted with the nurses there when something went wrong. About five minutes into the infusion of my fifth dose of Taxotere I began to notice that my upper lip was itchy. Within moments my entire mouth and chin area were itchy and my nose felt numb. I called for a nurse. There was one just a few chairs away and as soon as she looked at me she came running and stopped the infusion. I was having an allergic reaction to the drug!

She said my face was beet red and she immediately informed Dr. Powell. New orders were given. Within another few moments I was given Solu-Medrol through the IV, followed by Benadryl and Tagamet, all designed to arrest the allergic reaction. It worked. After waiting for the reaction to subside, the infusion could be restarted and it was completed, at a slower rate, without further incident.

This would, however, change the way my medication would be given each time. The Solu-Medrol, Benadryl and Tagamet preceded each dose of the Taxotere. This lengthened every treatment session by about 45 minutes, but there were no further reactions of that sort.

Left: Sarah and me during a treatment at the Hope Clinic.
Right: Earl, during one of the chemo sessions.

Dr. Powell's Staff

Everyone at the Hope Center was wonderful. The nurses, Katina, Cherie, Vickie and Kay, the ones I saw most often, were very helpful. They told me what to look for throughout the treatment and explained each new drug and its possible reactions in my system. They also observed carefully as the chemo was infusing, always ready to assist with the ever-present side effects or just to chat about how things were going.

The lab techs, Nancy and Stacey, performed the blood tests with accuracy and speed, and provided me with a copy of each report. Since I had a Medi-port they did not need to draw the blood, except on a couple of occasions when an additional sample was needed.

Judy greets everyone from the front desk, answers the phones and schedules all of my appointments. I'm sure she does much more than that as well, but just scheduling appointments would be a nightmare. There might be as many as five appointments to be made following one visit to the office, and that would be just mine! Imagine coordinating these matters for dozens of patients in a day!

The First Sign of Improvement!

At regular intervals Dr. Powell would order repeat blood work to track the progress of my therapy. There is a specific component that appears in the blood for most types of cancer called a tumor marker. In my case it was called CA 27.29, the marker for breast cancer. This was checked after about two months of therapy providing us with our first ray of hope. The normal value for someone who does not have breast cancer is 0-35. My number at diagnosis had been 2659.4, and this first test following therapy revealed that it had dropped to 1114.1, a decrease of 58%!

CT scans were also done every few months. The second of these provided us with more encouragement, showing that the largest of the tumors in the liver had decreased in diameter by 1.4 cm, more than ½ inch. Additionally, the Tumor Marker level had now dropped to 275.3. Was I *really* getting that much better? I didn't feel like it.

Though I felt worse than I had ever felt in my life, I had evidence that the chemo was working! I thought that with a little more endurance, perhaps this could be overcome.

But this was, after all, a medical marathon. The course was unfamiliar to me and I could not know for sure how far I'd come or how much further I must run. What would be next?

From my Journal:

We've settled into a routine again. Mom's got everything put away and some things ready for a garage sale.

Have had good news - the tumor markers dropped by 58%! But after 8 doses of chemo the first CT scan shows no change in the liver. We'll see Dr. Powell in 3 more days and see what he says about that.

Earl and I went to Bearcreek Farms in Bryant, Indiana for an overnight stay. Lots of quaint little stores to shop and a great bakery! Saw a musical revue called "California Dreamin" - 60's music. It was good, but exhausting. We cut our stay short. Had planned on two nights.

Chapter 10

Megan's "Locks of Love"

As it was still fairly cold from time to time and I was unaccustomed to being bald, I began wearing a hat everywhere. I had a hat by the door so I would not be caught by surprise and scare some stranger or friend with my pale, round face and bald head. I tried always to wear a hat when visitors were here, especially the grandchildren. The two grandsons, Drew and Riley were teenagers and had more understanding of what was happening. But the little girls, Megan and Hannah, were six and three and I was not sure how they would react to Grammie with no hair.

To my surprise, Megan who was nearly six when my cancer was diagnosed understood far more that we knew. On the drive back to Columbus after visiting here with her mother, she said, "I wish I could help Grammie. If my hair was black and curly, I would give her my hair."

Her mother was quite moved by Megan's compassion, and they talked about it at some length during the long drive home. Christy explained to her that while her hair was not like mine, there are also little girls who sometimes get sick and have to take medicine that makes their hair come out. Perhaps she could be of help to one of them.

Her big brown eyes widened and she said, "You mean I could help a child?"

"Yes."

"I want to do that!" she said with excitement in her voice. And when Christy asked if she realized her hair would no longer be long so it could be braided, Megan said, "It's just hair. It will grow."

Megan's hair was long and thick, like her mother's. Surely there was enough to donate for this cause. Christy promised to investigate it and they would discuss it again. She thought perhaps Megan would change her mind and she wanted to be sure she fully understood what would happen.

During the next few days they looked on the Internet and found an organization called "Locks of Love." There were several hairdressers in the Columbus area that worked with this group. The more she learned, the more determined Megan became. So an appointment was made and it was done, duly recorded with snapshots for the scrapbook. Eleven inches of beautiful brown hair was cut from Megan's head and she was left with chin-length hair.

They left the shop happy and satisfied that they would make a difference in some unfortunate child's life. At the time of this writing, her beautiful hair has already grown nearly as long as it was before and she is planning to donate it again in the coming summer months.

When she was five, little Hannah would do the same!

Chapter 11

Friends from the Kingdom Hall

After informing our immediate family members of this medical news, there was our larger, spiritual family to consider. As Jehovah's Witnesses, we not only have a great many friends here in our community but also have made friends with those "related to us in the faith" in many other areas.

Of course, our friends here in Lima have been much more available to lean on for support, and lean we have. No secrets here! We told them all what was happening.

Having always been the one who wanted to comfort others, yet now in need some comfort myself, I was free with information about how I was feeling and what was occurring. It seemed to me that if our friends knew what was happening they would be better able to help. Seeing that I was still on my feet and, for the most part still OK, *they* would feel better. And that made me feel better!

First there were the flowers, small gifts, cards and letters. News travels fast among people who truly love each other, and this was no exception. Soon I had mail from friends all over town, from nearby communities, and from as far away as Florida, Tennessee, Indiana, Michigan and of course Montana.

Our dearest friends, Jim and Mary, live in Montana where Mary grew up. When Jim retired, they moved there to be close to her parents and to be of help to them if possible.

We first met in 1971 when each of our families had two daughters. By 1977 we had each added a son to our family, the boys being born only two days apart. We always told the boys that they have been friends since before they were born! Nineteen months later we had Sarah, but they weren't about to try to keep the numbers even.

While we miss them dearly since their move out West, it provides us with the occasional opportunity to visit them there and see parts of the Rocky Mountain chain and Yellowstone National Park. I've always heard about people who "get sand in their shoes" after visiting the beach somewhere and always long to go back. Try getting an image of those magnificent Rocky Mountains in your memory and find out how you yearn to see them again!

"Meals on Wheels"

In addition to sending cards, our local friends banded together and decided to help in another significant way. By the third week of my treatments, I was given a calendar that had many of our friends' names on it. I was told that these dear people were going to bring us food on the day their name appeared on the calendar!

So, every Monday, Wednesday and Friday for more than a year, our evening meal was delivered to our door, ready to eat! In all there were 29 different sisters, as we call our female friends (and we are *just that close!*), who brought us dinner. Those calendars remain carefully tucked away with each name in place and the meal that was delivered written in beside the name. I will always remember these acts of love!

Husbands or children or grandchildren often accompanied many of these cherished friends as the meals were brought to our door. All of them demonstrated true Christian love in their efforts. Each one had received a copy of my special chemo diet so they prepared meals around the foods I could eat.

Beef and pork are not on that diet, so we had chicken several times every week, and prepared in more ways than I can count. Each meal was lovingly made ready and we always exchanged a few words and warm hugs as the food was brought. Occasionally we talked so long we had to reheat the food! But this regularly brought these dear friends into our home, which was very encouraging for me, especially during the long months that I was taking Taxotere.

"Is This Good?"

My real problem during this time was that most food had absolutely no flavor. It all tasted like cardboard to me. Earl and I would sit down to a lovely meal and after a few bites, I would ask, "Is this good?"

For some time, though he attempted to hide it from me, I could see that he was near tears as he answered. And it's not as though I wanted to make him feel bad that I could not taste the food, I really wanted to know! When I saw how it distressed him to realize that nothing had much flavor, I stopped asking. Occasionally he would inquire if something tasted good to me. And I must admit that occasionally I would fib just a little bit and say that it did. After all, that's what a good marriage is about... protecting one another from unnecessary pain.

Since I could not get out of the house most of the time, I busied myself with finding a way to sincerely thank our spiritual family for their loving gestures. I have several card-making programs on my computer, so each and every meal presentation was reciprocated with a proper "Thank You" card.

At first I simply printed enough cards for a month at a time and signed them. Then I decided that was not personal enough. So after a couple of months, I began personalizing the inside message for each individual. Sometimes it would have the individual's name printed, sometimes handwritten, but always hand signed with "Warm Christian love." That expression, meaningful as it is, does not fully convey our feelings.

Making those cards provided me with a way of expressing our gratitude for the help we were given and assisted in keeping my mind active when I could have just curled up on the couch and slept all my days away.

Does Anything Taste Good?

I found that frozen fruits and vegetables seemed to retain their flavor more than most other foods. Meat became difficult to eat, as I would nearly choke on it, no matter how long I chewed it. Fresh fruits and vegetables, other than those that could be peeled or scrubbed thoroughly, were not on the diet due to the possibility of contamination with bacteria and ensuing infection that low blood counts could not fend off. So, frozen or canned was the food of choice.

The one luxury on this diet was that I could have "any dessert not chocolate." Never in my life have I had that kind of freedom with desserts! I may have *acted* as though I did, but shouldn't have done so. In any case, we were also brought some of the most delicious and appealing desserts I have ever had!

From my Journal:

As fall approaches I am thankful for:

-The spring and summer I wasn't sure I would see.

-Our beautiful yard that Earl works so hard to keep that way, mowing, weeding, planting, fertilizing, etc.

-Jehovah's all-encompassing love.

-TUMOR MARKERS THAT CONTINUE TO DROP DRAMATICALLY EVERY TIME!! Now at 116.9

-Taxotere and Arimidex are working!

-Byron's clam chowder!

-I <u>still</u> have eyelashes... and eyebrows.

Chapter 12

Friends From Work

Work for nurses has always been pretty steady, as people are always getting ill or injured. Oh, there was a time in the mid-1970's when it was said that nurses were "a dime a dozen," and young people were encouraged to seek other occupations. That quickly became untrue. This aging and ill population is now in a nursing shortage of crisis proportions. Nurses of my age are or will be retiring soon, and there aren't enough new ones to replace us.

Most of my career as a nurse has been spent at the institution where I received my training as a nurse. It was a three-year Diploma program that provided its students with tremendous hands-on training. We were introduced to our future occupation early in our freshman year, and the time spent working at the hospital increased from half days as freshmen to working three and a half days as seniors. (In each case the remainder of the week was spent in class.) By the time of graduation, we had gained much confidence and looked forward to passing the State Board exam and being Registered Nurses.

During the mid-1960's, when I was in school, student nurses worked what today would be called a 'swing' shift, so that we had experience on all three shifts. We also were assigned to work a certain number of holidays. This broadened our experience and gave us a good overall perspective of the nurse's responsibilities at times other than when most physicians make rounds or are in their offices. And, of course, this was long before the days of pagers and cell phones that today make it somewhat easier to contact the doctor when you need him.

Living and working closely with classmates over three years creates a lasting bond. And in my case, continuing to live in the community where I went to school, I have been able to maintain communication with many other nurses that were in training at the same time. Quite a number of us continue to work and/or live in Lima.

Again, word travels fast, and when it became known that I had cancer, many of these old friends called or sent cards. Because nursing is so specialized today, and because my last two jobs kept me mostly confined to the area of the hospital where I worked, I had not seen or heard from many of these women for several years.

Their warm thoughts and wishes for recovery were well received and welcome. Some sent cards or phoned frequently, especially the friends from Utilization, Endoscopy, and IV Therapy. When you are suffering from a prolonged illness, it is amazing how much it helps to know that others genuinely care about you and are praying for your recovery! There were several instances where someone reported to me that *their* friends were praying for me! People I had never met and who didn't even know me! Amazing!

My friends from Utilization about once a month did one particularly encouraging thing. One of them would call and inquire if I might feel like meeting them for dinner at a local restaurant. Sometimes they would pick me up, or Earl would take me there and drop me off, since the use of Percocet prevented me from driving. Often I didn't feel like eating much and, just as it was at home, the food had little flavor for me. But I could catch up on the hospital happenings and what was new in the department. It was good to get out, despite the toll it took on my physical resources. The encouraging smiles and warm hugs made it more than worthwhile!

At the time of this writing, St. Rita's Alumni Association sponsored a recent dinner, attended by nearly 250 graduates of the school. Some who were there had graduated more than sixty years ago. My own class of 1966 had the largest representation, with nearly half of our 35 members present.

Chapter 13

Shop and Crop Till You Drop!

As time went on, I left the house only for medical treatments or to worship at our Kingdom Hall. I did not have enough energy for shopping, visiting or any other activities. But the meetings and treatments were making me better and I saved my energies for those occasions. Otherwise, Earl did all the shopping for groceries and other items that we needed. The remainder of the time, he was by my side.

Retail therapy, however, need not only be done in person! I discovered that I could shop at my leisure *on-line!* I could even shop in my jammies if I so desired, and I could shop at 2 in the morning or 2 in the afternoon. Soon we were getting catalogs from all sorts companies, and quite a few from companies we had never heard of before! Most of them had web addresses and their catalogs could be viewed on the computer. If I could figure out where to look on the web site, they might also have desirable items on sale or closeout. Soon we were getting packages in the mail or from the UPS deliveryman nearly every week, and sometimes several times a week!

My "mail-order therapy" brought some remarks from a couple of people about the UPS man knowing us by our first names, but I did not bother to elaborate on how exhausting it was to go to a store. Instead I went happily back to the computer and shopped some more.

It really is quite therapeutic!

Later when I began to feel somewhat stronger, I would make some trips to the store with my girls. I would call them especially if I needed to go to the scrapbook store. If my strength held up, we could wander the aisles of a store just looking at everything and nothing, something for which few men have the patience.

From my Journal:
Mom came over yesterday and folded nearly all the laundry that I did not get done on Monday. CHRISTY'S HOUSE IS UNDER CONTRACT!! NOW we're house hunting! Again!

More Family on the Move

As I mentioned earlier, three of our children were living and working in the Lima area. The fourth one had now acquired a local job and was commuting back and forth from Columbus, Ohio on weekends.

By summer that year Christy had settled into a routine. She came to Lima on Sunday evenings, worked all week at her new job, and then returned to Columbus on Fridays after work. One week Megan would come to Lima with her, spending her days with Papa and Grammie, and the next week she would stay in Columbus with her dad.

Christy began referring to her weekends as "sleepovers" with her husband! One Saturday they were at the grocery store and Darrin asked her if they needed to buy toothpaste.

She said, "I don't know. I'm only at your house on the weekends!"

Then she realized that if someone overheard that comment and looked at the three of them there in the store, that they might wonder what kind of relationship they have! After several months of searching, a suitable home was located here and the sale of the house in Columbus was completed. Before the first snowfall of the season they had moved. Soon they were settled in, the dogs were happy, and Megan was able to be with both of her parents all the time!

The Third Move is Completed

It was beginning to look like I would not be able to serve as the primary support person for Mom, after all. The first year of treatment was drawing close to an end, and my physical condition was anything but supportive for another person. I was doing well to support myself!

Ardy had been living in a small community about 50 miles from Lima. She and Wayne had moved there early in their marriage. His family was nearby and all of their children lived relatively close. But now, since his death in July of 2003, she felt a need to be closer to Mom and me. The big house in which they had raised their boys was too big for one person and held so many memories. She wanted some fresh surroundings.

The builder of Mom's condo had a home for sale right around the corner from her. It seemed a perfect fit for Ardy's needs and was so close their back yards almost met. By the end of 2004, on a cold, cloudy December day, the third member of my family moved to town and Ardy was also living in Lima. She soon became the principal driver for our mother.

Living so close, it was convenient for her to take Mom to her hair appointment or shopping for groceries. And, of course, there would be frequent visits to our house. It seemed that all of our arrangements were coming together well, and there was less to worry about.

Girls Just Gotta Have Fun!

It was sometime during that first summer of treatment I realized that I was not really doing anything for fun. I merely existed from treatment to treatment and from meeting to meeting at the Kingdom Hall. But I had a hobby that I was ignoring. My daughters and I have all made memory books or scrapbooks for several years. So I decided that they should all come here on Wednesday evenings and we could work on our scrapbooks together!

Admittedly, it was difficult to get started at first. My brain was so clouded much of the time that I just sat and looked at my things. I couldn't decide which pictures to work with or what items to use. I joked that I had "Scrapper's Block!" But my house was filled with laughter again and my family was around me every Wednesday.

Gradually I began to get more mentally organized, and I did two pages I called "Sometimes the Unexpected Happens." It includes pictures of everyone who came with me for chemo treatments, and me with no hair alongside my son who shaved his head in a gesture of solidarity and support! His words upon first seeing my thinning hair had been, "No hair is better than no Mom!"

Then I had an idea for a project. I had written some poetry in the past and several years ago our children had made a scrapbook for us based on the poem I wrote for Earl for our 32nd anniversary. Each child, including Mark, had done several stanzas of the poem in scrapbook form for the book. It was a wonderful surprise.

Scrappin' the Poetry

As I continued in my poetry writing, I had also written a poem for each child. I had poured my heart into the writing and started a year or more before this illness to make scrapbooks for the children. Each one would have pictures to go with the events mentioned in their poems. The projects had been put aside, however, falling victim to a busy work schedule and increasing tiredness.

Now I renewed my resolve to finish the books! I thought that if I did not survive this battle with cancer, at least each child would have his or her own poem, brought to life with pictures. I worked on them during the day when I knew the children would be at work, or during sleepless nights. There were more than a few occasions when one of them would drop by unexpectedly and I would have someone's scrapbook pages all over the kitchen table! I would frantically gather up the "incriminating" evidence and slip it into a drawer or under a newspaper, hoping not to be found out!

It worked. By November of 2004, they were finished. Christy had just completed her family's move to Lima earlier that month and invited everyone to her new home for a meal. It was the first time we had all been together in one house at the same time for sheer pleasure in many months.

I had wrapped the books carefully and after dinner presented each child with his or her book. There was silence for some time as the pages were perused, then laughter and tears as the pictures and decorated pages brought back memories of times past. They were all so pleased and I was so happy to have accomplished this labor of love. I had not been absolutely sure I would have time to complete it. But now it was done and the expressions on the faces of my children were reward enough. (See the poetry at p. 127)

From my Journal:

I WILL TRY NEVER TO TAKE FOR GRANTED:
-MY HUSBAND
-MY FAMILY
-JEHOVAH'S FRIENDS
-HOW GOOD A PIECE OF TOAST CAN BE
-SUNSHINE
-LAUGHTER
-FRESH FRUIT AND VEGETABLES

Chapter 14

Ice Age 2005!

The new year came and I was still in treatment. I had hoped that it would all be finished by February, but the closer that time came, the less it looked like I would be anywhere near the end of therapy. Dr. Powell's words had been that I was on chemo "indefinitely."

Then winter made a dramatic appearance. On Wednesday, January 5 an ice storm came through the area. This was not your everyday, run-of-the-mill winter storm. It dumped an inch and a half of ice (rain, sleet, freezing rain and snow) overnight and devastated the entire area! Trees and power lines were down everywhere resulting in 74,000 customers without electric service. Our electricity went off about 7:00 that evening. Two of the girls had just arrived for our usual scrapbook session when everything went dark.

We are somewhat accustomed to the power going off in our neighborhood. For whatever reason, it seems to do so fairly regularly. Our power lines are buried in this area, so it's usually a problem with the transformer in the middle of our block. Those outages are never fixed quickly. This one would be worse than we had experienced in our six years here in this neighborhood.

From my journal: New year. New regimen. All new drugs, almost. Overall there should be fewer side effects... and different ones.

Considering tumor ablation (it "cooks" tumors from the inside out with radio frequency) but must be cancer free everywhere but the liver to have it done. Hmmm.

No Lights, No Furnace

The scrapbook session was cut short as we searched for flashlights and candles. We hoped the power outage would not last long. We picked our way through the darkened house trying to remember what electric items had been on and turning them off so there would not be a huge drain on the power when it was restored.

By bedtime, we were still in the dark. So we bundled up and turned in, hoping to be awakened by the TV blaring or some bright light we might have forgotten to switch off. It didn't happen.

By morning it was pretty cool in the house. We have ventless gas logs in the fireplace so Earl turned them on to warm us up.

We also cook with gas, so while we couldn't have toast or bagels, we could light the stove with matches and have eggs or oatmeal and some coffee. We had checked in on the children by cell phone and found that remarkably, they all had power at first. So did Mother and Ardy.

As the day wore on, I was feeling weaker and more tired. By about noon that day, power was also out in the area where Mom and Ardy live. We knew they couldn't stay there without electricity, so they were invited to join us. At least we could all be warm. So Ardy put her little dog in the car, helped Mom pack some things, and the three of them came here.

Later we got word that a tree had fallen in Christy's yard severing her power line and her phone line. Her family was invited to stay with Sarah and her husband Tony, as their power was still on.

Soon Mark and Natalie's power was off, so they went to Angie and Steve's to bunk with them. We were relieved that everyone had a place to go, knowing that many throughout the area were in shelters or struggling to stay warm in their homes.

Pneumonia

As Thursday came and went, I was feeling worse and worse. By now we were spending the second night in our recliners in the living room closer to the fireplace. Mom and Ardy were sleeping on the couch and loveseat. The dogs slept at our feet. That night I was having trouble breathing. Not sure what was wrong, I had used my asthma inhalers but was not feeling better.

Here's where I made an error in judgment. Again, used to taking care of myself, I called the hospital's "Call-a-Nurse" number at 2:30 a.m. instead of calling Dr. Powell. Somehow, probably due to having been on call myself so many times, I must have reasoned that I didn't want to "bother" him in the middle of the night. Anyway, when I told the nurse that I was on chemo, a diabetic, short of breath from just walking to the bathroom from the living room, and having difficulty breathing even sitting there in my recliner, she advised me to come to the hospital right away.

By now it was 4 a.m. So, weak and exhausted and still in my pajamas, Earl and I got into the car. He drove around downed power lines as we carefully made our way to the hospital on the mostly deserted, ice-covered streets. By noon I had been stuck 4 or 5 times to have blood drawn (they couldn't get my Medi-port to give a blood sample!) and get an IV line in place, had my chest X-rayed, and had a CT scan done. It was decided that I had pneumonia.

The ER doctors had communicated with Dr. Powell by this time, however, and he did not want me admitted. That was good because there weren't any beds available. I was even placed in the hallway of the ER when I first arrived, as all of their rooms were full, too. The staff there, with whom I had worked, told me they were even diverting all the ambulances to the hospital across town because there was no place to put anyone!

I was discharged to home with an antibiotic and instructions to take aerosol (breathing) treatments every six hours. We had as a power source a glorified car battery on wheels that we had been using to operate the pumps on our marine aquarium to try to keep the fish and corals alive, to keep one light on when it was dark, and now to operate my nebulizer or breathing machine.

We found that it would run for about eight hours with those things in use, and then it needed a recharge. Steve or Mark would come and get it and recharge it at Angie and Steve's, which took about six hours. This was getting complicated. I felt as though it was an added burden on everyone.

Meanwhile, everything in our refrigerator freezer thawed out and was lost. Family members were getting bread and milk for us, or picking up prescriptions, etc. We were storing items in a cooler with ice. We feared for the contents of the deep freeze in the garage, although it would stay frozen longer there.

We were keeping up with the news by means of a battery-powered radio. This storm was the worst in many years and worse locally than most other areas around us.

The dogs fared better than the rest of us. They wore their "coats" all the time and were never really uncomfortable! But the stress was beginning to have an effect on Mom. The frequent phone calls and people coming and going making the dogs bark were taking a toll on her nerves. She missed the calm quietness of her own home.

Power Up!

On Saturday morning Earl made a trip to a local hardware retailer for supplies to repair a leaky water line in our bathroom. (Don't those things always happen at the most inopportune time?) On his way into the store he passed a number of people coming out of the store with gas-powered generators on carts. As he got inside, he saw another ten or so customers waiting in line who also had generators. A clerk told him that they had received a shipment of two truckloads of generators. They were over $500 each.

He came home with his plumbing purchase and we talked about the generators. We still had no idea how long the power would be off, and it was tiring and time-consuming for the boys to lug our battery back and forth for charging. We decided that it would be $500 well spent, much like an insurance policy against future outages. By the time he got back to the store within an hour or so nearly half of the generators were already sold. We were glad he went when he did.

A friend of ours, another of the elders in our congregation who lives fairly close, is an electrician by trade. So Earl phoned to see if he could help with hooking up the new appliance. Dick soon arrived with a cable and his expert knowledge.

Christy, known as "Dad's oldest son" because she always helped with his projects, had already taken the thing out of its box and attached the wheels. Meanwhile her dad was doing the bathroom repair job. It needed to be done while there was still daylight.

Shortly we heard the rat-a-tat of the generator running in the driveway! Within minutes we had lights in several rooms and we heard the refrigerator kick on and the furnace fire up. We were living large now!

Finally I could take my breathing treatments without wondering whether the power would last long enough to finish it, or if the boys would get the recharged battery back in time for the next one.

But Mom was not faring well. She continued to sleep sitting up on the loveseat, and we could see that she needed some real "quiet time." There was a continual parade of people coming and going and the phone ringing as family and friends checked to see if there was anything else that could be done for us. She was used to being alone with her own things around her and we recognized how truly distressing this whole situation was to her. We kept hoping for a resolution.

By Sunday afternoon the power was back on in the condos and Mom and Ardy could return to their own homes. The game of "musical chairs" came to mind as the children continued to swap dwelling places over the next few days. Power would be restored in one neighborhood and go out in another. Finally on Tuesday afternoon our power came back up. What a luxury to have everyone in their own homes with lights and heat and appliances that worked!

We endeavor not to take these things for granted, but often don't realize how fortunate we are until our luxuries are taken away for a while. It had not been easy "camping out" in our living room, but we all survived.

Chapter 15

Tumbling Tumor Markers

One of the tools of today's Oncologist is the tracking of a patient's progress by periodic testing of the Tumor Marker for that patient's particular type of cancer. Mine, as mentioned previously, is the CA 27.29. The normal range, for someone who does not have breast cancer is 0-38.4. At the time of my diagnosis, my CA 27.29 was 2658.4.

By late April it had fallen to 1114.1, and we were elated that the chemo was working! A month later, it was 772.8, and by July it had dropped to 275.3. In August it was 116.9, less than half of the count of just the previous month. We continued to be optimistic, though the CT scans were less encouraging. A scan in July 2004 showed the largest of the liver tumors to be reduced in size, but subsequent scans would invariably report "Hepatic lesions unchanged from previous scan." And so began the disparity between the Tumor Markers and CT scan results. The best news was that there were no new lesions. At least my condition was not worsening.

Through the continuing months of chemotherapy, we waited anxiously for the Tumor Marker report that would be done each month. The first elevation in number occurred in October. I was devastated and felt sure that the chemo was no longer working, even though the increase was only by three and a half points. In my mind, it could be the beginning of the end and I imagined a steady deterioration of my condition.

Dr. Powell assured me that this was such a small increase that there could be a variation of that amount from one blood sample to another on consecutive days, or that even being slightly dehydrated could make that much difference. By December it was down again, to 70.9 and I felt much better about the treatments.

Dr. Powell, however, was ready for a change.

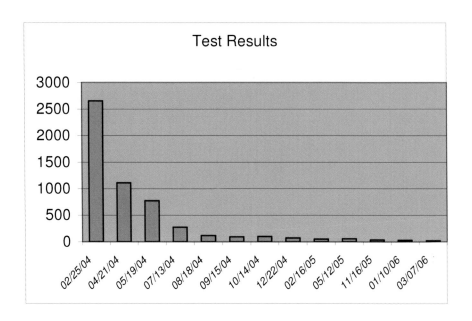

"Just Because You're Paranoid Doesn't Mean They're Not After You!"

We waited with anxious concern to see what the next tumor marker report and CT scan would show. To our dismay, the tumor marker increased again and the CT scan showed "No change." Dr. Powell told us that a different laboratory was now doing the CA27.29 test, as the old one had been bought out.

He said, "We might be comparing apples to oranges," if the new lab used a different "assay" or method of evaluation. He had earlier told us that tumors many times die from the inside out and that the outer shape may not reflect that change for a long time. This could account for the CT scan results. We could only hope that was the case now.

Still, it did little to calm my nerves. My paranoia was showing again and, as Dr. Powell himself had said once, "Just because you're paranoid doesn't mean they aren't after you!"

Additionally, the next CT scan gave us no new information. A different Radiologist had read each one that had been done and we were beginning to feel that there might be no continuity there.

Dr. Powell called the Radiologist's office while we were there in the room and told the person on the other end of the line, "I want to know, is this better or is it worse? And I don't want a hedge! I want him to call me and explain this reading because it doesn't tell me anything. This patient's treatment depends on the results of this scan and I need to know!"

I felt good about his reaction. I needed a persistent, dynamic coach in this marathon, and that's what I had in Dr. Powell.

 **From my Journal**: *Still can't breathe well and have an awful rash under my breasts & around my waist. Am getting Neulasta nearly every week and it gives me MASSIVE headaches. Ran into the foot of the bed last night in the dark and broke 3 toes!! Now it is really difficult to walk!*

Food is beginning to taste better!

Saw the podiatrist today and he removed both great toenails. Should have new nails by the end of the year!

Dr. Powell Selects Another Drug

After ten months on Taxotere, the side effects were mounting almost unbearably. I was battling nearly every side effect listed for Taxotere! The Tumor Marker, CA 27.29 was at 70.9, admittedly a very dramatic change from the 2658.4 the first time it was checked. However, over the past three months it had been up and down and back up again, and the rapid progress that had been occurring early on was no longer being seen. Something different needed to be done.

Again we relied on Dr. Powell's expertise.

He selected an older drug used for breast cancer, Doxil. It is actually a newer form of an older drug and he felt it would bring the results we desired. Doxil would be given on a three-week cycle of one week of therapy and two weeks off.

The prospect of no longer suffering from the side effects that had taken over my life was inviting! I looked forward to this new treatment with renewed enthusiasm. At the same time, I knew that I was continuing to exist only because of the effect of the Taxotere on my cancer. My paranoia was showing!

It turned out to be a pleasant change from the previous drug and I would soon see remarkable changes in the way I was feeling. More than that, food began to have some flavor for me again! This would prove to bring mixed blessings, as the better the food tasted, the more I ate! I had lost fifty pounds during the "cardboard-flavored, relentless diarrhea" phase. On this new regimen I would regain forty of those pounds. That was discouraging.

What Is Next?

Within about six weeks, I was beginning to lose much of the extra fluid in my system, and the "chipmunk" face was going away. I had more energy. Gradually over several months I saw that the face looking back at me from the mirror was beginning to look familiar again!

Along with these good things came a few new side effects, different from before. Doxil produces an effect called "PPE" which stands for a really complicated term that means the palms of your hands and the soles of your feet will get very red and the skin will peel! It did. Also, there is the potential for heart damage, so a baseline echocardiogram was done at the beginning of treatment, and repeated every two months or so.

From My Journal:
Skin rash persists & itches even during the night. Saw the dermatologist.

Skin on my hands and feet peels and they are very sensitive. The skin is so thin and shiny it appears that I would almost have no fingerprints!

Read recently, in treatment for cancer "There is radiation therapy, chemotherapy, and RETAIL THERAPY!" How true!

I am researching breast surgeries and plastic surgeons. One type of reconstructive surgery involves also getting a 'tummy tuck!' Maybe there will be a benefit! ☺

Chapter 16

Hair

Along with the new side effects to Doxil, a surprising thing happened. My hair began to grow again! The new hair growth was somewhat disappointing at first. Where my hair had been black with scattered strands of silvery-gray, what was growing now was all gray. And while Earl always said he loved those silvery strands, I feared that it would remain entirely gray and was not sure *I* was ready for that!

Maybe he wouldn't like *all* of it gray. I was really feeling old. Perhaps I would have to resort to coloring it! I had always resisted the impulse to do that, feeling that I had *earned* those gray hairs. Besides, my father had never allowed any of us girls to color our hair when we lived at home, and Earl had never wanted me to color it before now. I figured that opinion hadn't changed.

But as more and more hair grew, the remainder of the new growth was all black, so that now I have only slightly more gray than I had before the chemo. And, as often happens after chemotherapy, it is so curly it looks as though I have had a perm! Angie even thought I had. Suddenly the color was not so important after all. It was hair growing from my head!

Bretta and the Family

Speaking of hair, I must tell you about my hairdresser! Bretta Roush owns her shop and has half a dozen or so employees who work for her. For twelve years or so she has been cutting my hair and giving me a perm regularly. Over the years we have become close friends, confiding in one another our life events.

Two of my three daughters also go to Bretta's shop for their hair care, as well as my daughter-in-law, two of my granddaughters, my sister and my mom. It has become a real family affair, and she seems to love all of us as much as we love her.

For the past four years the shop has had a "Breast Cancer Awareness" program that coincides with the national Awareness program in October each year. Pink "ribbons" can be purchased and the walls are decorated with them, each one adorned with the name of a breast cancer patient past or present.

One week during the 2005 promotion they had a bake sale. Another year a cookbook of customers' favorite recipes was compiled and sold. During this time Bretta's little shop has raised over $10,000 for breast cancer! Some of it is allocated for research, but most of it stays right here in our community to assist cancer patients with their needs. Every cent raised is donated for this cause.

When Bretta learned that I had cancer, she was floored. There were hugs and tears. And from the day that she received that information, she would not allow me to pay her to cut my hair! "It's nothing," she would say. "Just a little snip here and there. I want to do this for you!" (Soon after I entered remission, I insisted on paying for her services again.)

Cut it Short... No, Give Me A Buzz!

When my hair began to fall out rapidly just before the Symphony event, I called Bretta for an appointment. I wanted it all cut very short. I thought that extremely thin hair would look best if it was at least all the same length and very short. So that was accomplished while Earl was on his way to Florida to get Mom.

Within a few days I decided it was still too long and enlisted my sister's help with our dog clippers. (In her first career she had been a hairdresser.) After reassuring her that I would not be upset no matter the result, she gave me a buzz, and the hair was gone.

The hair loss had not been unexpected, given the fact that it is a common side effect of chemo. What I had not considered was that the hair we often don't even notice would also be gone. I soon discovered that there was no hair on my arms, no hair on my legs or armpits (At last, a vacation from shaving!), no hair on my chin (I *HATE* those!), and no hair *in my nose!* Who would have thought of that?! (See previous information on side effects and nose running!) No hair **ANYWHERE**. Now, that was strange!

From my Journal:

Eyebrows and lashes are gone now. Fingernails look awful with multiple layers of nail, very dark on the right hand, irregular on the surface and around the edges. They are elevated from the nail bed. I have trimmed away as much as possible so as to avoid catching them on everything. Some days I wear band-aids on 4 or 5 fingers to protect the nails. Numbness in the fingertips persists despite the Vit. B6.

Hats Off!

As mentioned previously, I had purchased several hats through a mail-order catalogue from the American Cancer Society provided by my nurse-friend, Sharon. Over time another order was sent and other hats were purchased locally. Some were for summer wear and some were for cold weather. Some were hand made by my husband's cousin and arrived unexpectedly in the mail, friends or family gave others to me. Angie hand-knit one hat for me that I always wore to bed. It's incredible how cold your head is at night without hair, especially during winter months!

Soon I had quite a collection of hats. There were casual hats and hats for wearing to the Kingdom Hall. Hats to block all the summer sun and others to allow a gentle breeze through.

One evening Sarah came over and decided that she needed to go to Wal-Mart for something. Would Natalie and I like to go along? By this time I was ready for an occasional outing and I always enjoyed being with the girls. So we piled into Sarah's car and off we went. As she was pulling into the parking space I realized I had forgotten to put on a hat! My hair had begun to grow back, but it was still very sparse.

"Oh, Sarah," I said. "I'll have to wait in the car."

"Why?" she asked.

"I forgot my hat!" I exclaimed. "I can't go in there without a hat!"

"Sure you can," she said. "Your hair is growing and it looks fine! It's your 'Battle Scar.' Make this your 'coming out' without a hat!"

Natalie concurred, and I deferred.

"OK, but we have to go straight to the hat department and get a hat first. Then I'll do some shopping."

So, off we went, into Wal-Mart with my half-a-head of hair! I was sure everyone would stare at the funny-looking little fat woman with hardly any hair. But if they stared, I didn't notice. I avoided making eye contact with anyone.

We quickly arrived in the hat department and the search began.

"Here, Mom, try this one on!" Sarah said, holding out what looked like a furry, pink version of a mail carrier's winter hat with the ear covers pulled down.

"No!"

"Oh, please. It'll be fun!" she said.

Obediently I donned the hat and we all melted into laughter. Natalie also tried it on resulting in more laughing! Finally, after a bit more foolishness and some trial and error, I settled on a pink faux-suede newsboy type hat. I tucked the tags inside, put it on and wore it through the rest of the store, confident that no one would be staring now unless we were too loud with our laughter.

At the checkout, I addressed the clerk.

"I'm going to take this hat off long enough for you to scan it and then I want to wear it again. I left home without my hat and I haven't been out in public without one in over a year."

"I understand," she replied. "I lost my hair, too, but it's been five years now and I'm doing well."

Here was another involuntary member of "the club" in our midst and we would never have known if I hadn't gone out without my hat!

The Photo Shoot

Near the beginning of summer in 2005, Sarah came to the house with her camera. We planned a photo shoot with all of my hats! Out on the deck, I would put one of the hats on, and she would take a picture. I would change hats and change position, and she would take another picture.

I posed for her as though I was a model, round face and all, and we laughed uproariously. I posed with each of our two dogs. I posed on the swing on the deck. I posed with a softball bat, in the ball caps of course... batting right <u>and</u> left! (No competition for former

Cleveland shortstop Omar Vizquel!) In the end, when I had worn all 25 hats… yes, there are that many!… she stacked them all up on my head and we called the final shots "The Mad Hatter!" It's difficult to balance that many hats at once, especially when you're rolling with laughter!

What a delightful daughter she is who can make her sick old mother act silly and laugh till her sides hurt!

Laughter *is* good medicine.

Hannah Fisher, age 5, wearing one of Grammie's hats.

Baby Miranda, Age 4 months, wearing one of Hannah's hats.

Natalie

Daughter Sarah

Me again

Wigs!

Speaking of laughter, just about the time I was changing chemo drugs, before I knew that my hair would begin to grow again so soon, my friend Dolly offered to take me wig shopping. I knew they were available, but had been satisfied until now with my hats. Not knowing how much longer I would need head coverings, and being pretty sure Earl would not enjoy shopping for a wig with me, I decided to take Dolly up on her offer.

On a cold day in January 2005 we set out for a wig store in a local mall.

I was amazed at what I saw! Every color or mix of colors imaginable was there in any length one could possibly want. I decided to stay with a color and length similar to what my natural hair had been, a sort of salt-and-pepper blend with more pepper than salt when it disappeared.

The woman who worked in the store allowed me to try on some of the wigs. After selecting two, I cautiously removed my hat and quickly donned one of the hair pieces, happy that there were no other shoppers nearby and that we were in the back of the store.

'Not bad,' I thought wearing the first one. But after so many months of having NO hair, it seemed like too much hair. It was longer than I had worn my hair in years, and really seemed too artificial, although I liked the color. It was a mix of black and gray, with perhaps more gray than I'd had.

The next one was cut shorter. The style was closer to my head and more nearly the style I had worn before it all went down the drain. And this one was natural hair. The "cap" of it was also more comfortable. This one, however, was more dark brown with some lighter highlights, not really my color. What to do? Well, I got them both!!

So Dolly and I left with the purchases over my arm… in their bag! Soon our friends began making statements such as, "How nice that your hair is growing back!" I didn't always tell them that I hadn't *grown* it. I did, after all, *own* it!

More of Sarah's Shenanigans!

One evening when we were having our weekly "Scrap Night," I suddenly became much too warm and reached up and whipped off my wig!

"Whew! That's better!" I sighed as the cooler air swirled around my nearly bare head. The night before this I had also removed the wig in the throes of an internal power surge and Hannah had picked it up and put it on. I had quickly snapped a couple of pictures (Who doesn't have a camera handy with grandchildren in the house?) and she had turned around, patting the back of the wig as a model might. Suddenly the memory of the shots inspired Sarah.

"Hey Natalie!" she said. "Try Mom's wig on!"

Just as it had happened in the Wal-Mart store with the hats, she put it on and uproarious laughter ensued. Then Sarah put it on over her own long blonde hair and the sidesplitting howls began anew as she posed this way and that while I snapped away.

"Angie! You do it!" She grabbed the digital camera and continued snapping between gales of laughter. Soon the wig had made the rounds of everyone in the house, including Earl and two-month-old Miranda!

The giggles were invigorating and we were all holding our sides. Each person made appropriately amusing faces and posed ridiculously for the overall effect. More than one person present that evening declared they had nearly had laundry problems! Trying the same wig on lots of people is not recommended on a full bladder!

The following Monday the laughter began anew as my sons-in-law were added to the gallery of wig shots. Appropriately, this "photo-shoot" became the subject of scrapbook pages in several of our books!

Recently I read that five seconds of good belly laughing is as healthy for us as a fifteen-minute walk. I figure my family has provided me with the equivalent of several half-hour jogs!

Chapter 17

The Tumor Board

The Tumor Marker report was continuing to reflect up and down results. The CT scans were inconclusive and both of these seemed to conflict with what Dr. Powell was seeing clinically. Still we had no solid evidence on which to base any conclusions about my therapy.

In June 2005, Dr. Powell took my case to the hospital's Tumor Board as he had done early in my therapy. He had explained to us then that the Board meets monthly and physicians who are treating cancer patients may go there to present a new case or one with which they may be having problems.

When the case is presented the other oncologists there offer opinions on other therapies or treatments that could be tried. It's like getting a second and/or third opinion without ever seeing another physician. There were four other oncologists there the first time my case had been presented and they all concurred on the treatment that Dr. Powell had selected.

But now he described me as an "enigma." None of the tests agreed with each other and he could draw no firm conclusions from the scans, blood work and the physical exams.

"So what did the other oncologists think?" I asked at the next visit.

They said, "You've *already* done more than *we* would have!" he told me.

This was incredible to me! "So, they would have given up?"

The answer was, "Yes."

"Well," I replied, "I'm certainly happy that I came <u>here</u>!"

He assured me that not only did he have another therapy to try but he also had others in mind if that failed. Once again, I was sure I had made the right choice in this man.

Over the next nine months, my finger and toenails began to heal beautifully, my hair began to grow again and I sensation was returning in my fingertips and feet. Now my fingertips were so sensitive in fact that I could no longer stand the pain inflicted by the lancets needed to check my blood sugar each day. How much longer would this marathon last? Just where was the finish line?

'Cat' Scan, 'Dolphin Scan,' PET Scan!

Dr. Powell had ordered a PET (Positron Emission Tomography) scan in April. These are really high-tech scans, done after an injection of radioactive glucose. The most active cells in your body, presumably cancer cells, grab up the glucose and "glow" on the films. In my case, the first test yielded no new information due to the therapeutic effect of Neulasta, which stimulates the bone marrow to produce white blood cells. The only thing that "lit up" was bone, but I had no symptoms of bone cancer. So he decided to repeat it as soon as the insurance company would allow.

That time came in late September 2005. Although we took great care not to have any Neulasta or Aranesp (again, it stimulates bone marrow, but this drug aids in production of red blood cells) in my system this time, the results were still inconclusive. What to do?

When I saw Dr. Powell the following week and he gave me the test results, he said, "I don't want to keep you on chemo forever. The only way to really know what's going on is to get a direct look at the tissue. I think it's time to get that tumor out of there." I agreed.

Then he added, "You won't like me for this, but I think we need another liver biopsy to see what's going on in there, too."

The memory of the previous one was no longer fresh and I chose not to attempt to refresh it. However, I was tiring of continued treatment and not knowing absolutely what was happening. Again, I agreed. I was ready to try almost anything if it meant getting off of chemo.

"This will be your last chemo at least until after your surgery," he said. I went to the treatment room for one more dose of Doxil.

Finally I would be *sure* that the cancerous lump that had started this whole nightmare would be gone! Never have I looked forward to surgery with so much eager anticipation! At the beginning of treatment the prospect of surgery was so remote, being 'perhaps not necessary.' Even talking about surgery now meant that my situation was entirely changed. Though I had never lost hope, it was now renewed with even more vigor. And it was to be a lumpectomy, not mastectomy! At least for now, I could keep both of my breasts!

From my Journal:

I am more moody and irritable lately. I had made up my mind that this (surgery) would happen last year. And when Dr. P. kept saying surgery would be "of no benefit" and would "delay treatment with chemo" and even "might be unnecessary," I gradually put it out of my thoughts. Now he says it's necessary and I'm having trouble with that! It's hard to wrap my brain around.

On the other hand I am happy because:

-MY HAIR HAS GROWN SO MUCH I HAD TO GET IT CUT!
-I HAVE ALMOST ENTIRELY STOPPED WEARING HATS!
-FOOD TASSTES GOOD AGAIN!! *(That could be a problem!)*
-I HAVE GREATLY REDUCED MY PERCOCET CONSUMPTION
-JEHOVAH IS MY SHEPHERD (Ps. 23)
-I HAVE MORE ENERGY
-MY NEW HAIR IS CURLY!!

-My eyebrows are half grown back and I have at least a dozen eyelashes!

Chapter 18

Another Heartbreak

As if it were not enough to be fighting cancer, another event occurred that left us feeling as though we'd all had the wind knocked out of us. Our world was turned upside down.

It came on the heels of what should have been the one bright spot early in my second year of treatment. Our fifth grandchild was born in February of 2005, another beautiful girl who would be named Miranda Sue Ann Fisher. (Sue being my middle name and Ann being the middle name of Natalie's mother.)

But, times being what they are, her father had grown restless. What should have been a happy home was anything but that. By the time Miranda was two weeks old she was living with Papa and Grammie along with her mother and sister. This was at our invitation and a decision we would never regret other than the reason for its necessity.

Natalie needed help with the children and could not manage by herself. So, two weeks after her caesarean section, she was settled in our guest room with her new baby and Hannah. Though it was crowded there, across the hall she had the assistance that she required and at least some solace for her wounded emotions.

How would this work out for us? I needed a nap every day and was barely able to keep up with the things I needed to do. What would it be like with toys everywhere and three more people in the house all the time?

This is what it was like. Hannah once more became the delight of our lives despite her confusion, frustration and occasional anger. Her incessant questions and lilting voice brought smiles to our faces every day, helping to bring us out of our sorrow.

Admittedly, there were nights when little Miranda was fussy and Natalie, exhausted and fresh from her C-Section, could not console her. It can be frustrating to hear a baby cry, especially when you are ill yourself. After a long day of chasing Hannah and nursing the baby Natalie's energy levels bottomed out. Could I possibly be of help?

Grammie and the Baby

Yes! Someone needed *me* and I could be on the giving end again! Now when my nights were sleepless I would peek into the study where Natalie often slept in the recliner with her new daughter. I would shuffle into the room and offer my help. It was then that we often had long middle-of-the-night conversations after which I could take that tiny baby in my arms and hold her close until she needed to be nursed again.

Miranda and I slept in my recliner, the long hours passed, and we bonded while Natalie got some much-needed, uninterrupted sleep. We kept up this routine, switching off the tiny bundle between mother and grandmother, and Miranda grew and the mother and grandmother healed.

In early April when Natalie had recovered from the surgery sufficiently to drive and the weather was better, she took the girls to visit her parents in Tiffin. They were gone for parts of four days. During that time my blood count was down and I was exhausted. I spent most of those four days on the couch again.

"It's Like Getting My Own Baby Back!"

Upon their return late that Thursday, I was still on the couch, feeling weak and tired. Uncharacteristically, I had not even gotten up when the three arrived. Natalie called me to the bedroom to look at Miranda. She seemed to have a rash of some sort and she wanted nurse/Grammie to look at it.

I dragged myself off the couch and into the room. As I examined the offending pink spots on her chest I reached out to touch a tiny hand and suddenly my heart ached to hold this baby again! It was as though someone had taken my own child away from me and now she was back!

Perhaps the rash was from a change in water if some of her clothes had been washed in Tiffin. It didn't matter. I was impatient to pick her up and could barely wait to get her sleeper on her! I quickly closed the snaps, clutched her to my breast and carried her to the living room. I could not believe how much I had missed this baby!

She had done it. This now eight-pound bundle of smiles and diapers and baby smells had me completely in her clutches. And it was precisely where I wanted to be!

The Therapeutic Baby

In the following months we began to refer to Miranda as the "therapeutic baby." The bigger she got and the more progress she made as she grew, the better I felt. My strength was returning and I needed it to keep up with her.

As she progressed from coos and smiles to full grins of recognition, Grammie continued to get stronger. Soon Miranda, or "Randi" as Papa nicknamed her, was crawling and into everything within her reach, and I had replaced my Percocet with Extra Strength Tylenol. As she grew I was gaining strength and it no longer tired me easily to pick her up countless times throughout the day.

Miranda pulled herself up for the first time!

Natalie eventually got an early morning job, arising at 4:15 A.M. to stock shelves at a local retailer, while the breakfast chores for the girls fell to me. So it was that I was first to see little Randi *standing up* in her crib when I went to get her one morning! Other firsts were reached while she was here... first tooth and first steps. Seeing the faces of those beautiful little girls first thing in the morning brought us such joy!

And Then There Were Two

But, as surely as I was healing both physically and emotionally (as far as that could be accomplished while still estranged from Mark), so was Natalie. So by the end of October, she had found an apartment for herself and her girls. Would they be OK? How would she manage without us?

Quite well, as it turns out. Her work schedule changed so that she need not be gone during those early morning hours unless the girls were visiting with Mark. Or she could still spend an occasional night here and we could again have a fun breakfast with the girls.

Thus another chapter in our lives drew to a close, however reluctantly on our part. We knew, of course, that day would have come eventually. But we could never have chosen the day. It would have been impossible to decide upon the day that we would no longer wake up with those cheerful little voices and happy faces to brighten our days.

So here we are again. Just the two of us. We still see the girls several times each week, but it will never be the same. Their being here, however briefly, has enriched our lives. We have developed a bond with them that is so special and precious to us both.

 **From my Journal**: *Mark went to a local university for one quarter and part of the second quarter. He made the Dean's List. We were so proud of him! We got that information only a couple of weeks before Natalie and the girls moved here.*

-What AGONIZING pain this broken marriage causes. It is easier to deal with cancer...

-MIRANDA CHEERS ME UP EVERY DAY!

Grammie and the "Therapeutic Baby"

Miranda at age 3 above, age 5 below

Chapter 19

Hitting the Wall

There is a point in a marathon race, I am told, when every runner feels he just cannot go on. When the body has burned all of the available carbohydrates and cannot use the fats, pain increases and the pace of the runner slows dramatically. This is called "hitting the wall." Many factors contribute to this, including the runner's mental and emotional conditioning, training, and preparation for this particular race.

I had reached that point in my race. I hit the wall.

I felt as though I would be on chemo forever, that I would never have energy again. I felt that my family was falling apart. I even grieved somewhat over my career as a nurse being cut short. I also worried that this illness might deplete our financial resources.

But in all this time I never really thought about how I was coping emotionally with this. I was too busy with treatments and medications, or trying to combat the side effects of the treatment or the actual symptoms of cancer. Or trying to cope with the heartache that results from broken families.

Looking back, I recognize that during the darkest days in the beginning of treatment and again at the beginning of 2005 I suffered with clinical depression. Though I do not recommend delaying treatment, I did not seek treatment until late summer of 2005. I felt I should be able to "deal" with it. After all, I am the nurse! I help others, so surely I should be able to help myself!

I was wrong.

Several times I suffered what I referred to as a "meltdown." The first day that this happened was a Saturday morning in early summer of 2004. Mark had come by the house when he got off work at 11 a.m. I had been crying in the bedroom. When I thought I had composed myself, I joined Mark and Earl at the table in our kitchen. But the tears again ran uncontrollably. I could not stop them if I tried. I had made a mental estimate of no less than a year of therapy from the beginning of my treatment and I knew this was much too early to be "tired of being sick." Yet that was how I felt.

I was used to full days of activity, getting up early and working hard most days. I was *not* used to lying around day after day with barely enough strength to get off of the couch!

There would be several more bad days before I fully accepted the need for help.

Talking About It

I finally sought some therapy. The journey began with a visit to Dr. Powell, then by means of a referral to a psychologist. Through a number of discussions with Dr. Frederick Ferri, I began to think about how all of this had affected me, from the actual illness itself to my family members and their own individual problems. And I accepted the offer of medication to assist with this healing, as I had the medication that helped me heal physically.

When I thought that this disease might have been discovered earlier, I was mildly upset. But I had saved my energy for fighting the illness rather than directing it in anger. Mostly I wondered how long it really had been present and how much less I might have suffered if it had been found sooner.

Through it all I learned that I am very much loved! For much of my life I had felt that I just didn't "fit in" in most situations and places. But since this illness appeared, I had been hearing from family and some friends for the first time in many years. (I have a large basket *stuffed* with cards and letters!)

I figured out that not many things in life matter much if you have your faith, good family and friends, and your health. In that order. Returning to work was very low on my priority list. Spending time in worship and with my family has the number one spot on that list.

I realized that where formerly I had expected to become a very old woman beside the love of my youth, then thought those dreams would be cut short by a considerable length of time, now that prospect seemed to be within reach again. I have faced breast cancer and walked away... with both of my breasts!

Chapter 20

Is it Gone?

In researching mastectomy and reconstructive surgery I had contacted a center located in New Orleans, LA where a progressive new surgery is performed. It avoids use of abdominal muscle during the reconstructive process and has a shorter healing time. I had just received a folder from them when hurricane Katrina devastated the area. I had to assume that the center there was destroyed along with a great deal of that beautiful city. Although many others might miss the services of that center, it turned out that I wouldn't!

It was about that time that Dr. Powell had the second PET scan performed with its still inconclusive results. The tumor markers had increased again and the most recent breast ultrasound indicated that the tumor there was slightly enlarged.

It was then that he scheduled the surgery and a second liver biopsy. His recommendation was for lumpectomy. Again, I visited Dr. Olt. After her examination, she scheduled the procedure.

The day of surgery came at last, October 6, 2005. Earl and I arrived at 7:45 for the insertion of the guidewire that would direct Dr. Olt to the tumor.

Later some dye was injected for the sentinel node biopsy. That procedure was more than a little uncomfortable. The radioactive blue dye was injected at two sites, one at the tumor site and one through the nipple. (Ouch!) The dye moves through the lymphatic system and the surgeon tracks it to the first or "sentinel" node, which is then removed for examination by a pathologist. The dye also made a large blue spot appear on the skin. (Nearly one year later I am still "part Smurf" as the dye has not gone completely away!)

I moved through the familiar formalities of paperwork, this time in the Outpatient Surgery department. Again, many individuals with whom I had worked over the years were there and I could not have asked for a friendlier group to provide my care. Even my former roommate from nurses training was there and she came to my room with warm greetings and a hug. She had undergone a double mastectomy herself about a year previous to this and here she was back at work! I admired her stamina and endurance.

My pre-op room was filled with family! All three of my girls were there with Earl, as well as my mom and Ardy. I had brought my own support group! Our prayers were said silently as we waited for the appointed time to arrive.

In the holding area we spoke with the anesthesiologist and Dr. Olt. Finally it was time to go, and Earl was directed to the waiting room.

As I was wheeled into the operating suite I could only think how odd it seemed to be in that sterile environment without wearing a surgical mask! Early in my career as a nurse I had spent about four years working in surgery and I felt as though I should be wearing a mask like everyone else.

Soon another kind of mask was put over my face to give me a little "oxygen," or so they said. I remember commenting that it smelled good. Next some medication was injected through my IV, and that is the last thing I remember until I was in the recovery room.

I'm Clever, Even Under Anesthesia!

Dr. Olt had said that if she removed only the lump and the sentinel lymph node the surgery would take 45 minutes or so, perhaps an hour. If more surgery were required, it would take longer. I was scheduled for surgery at 1:00.

When I became aware that I was in the recovery area and had the ability to think somewhat clearly, I wondered how much surgery had been done. In my fog, I thought that the only thing the nurses there could tell me is, "Your surgery is over." So a thought occurred to me through my foggy brain that I perceived to be rather clever!

"What time is it?" I asked.

The reply came back, "Ten minutes after 3:00."

Now I was worried. Surgery had taken nearly two hours!

I was given some medication for pain and slept again. After the prescribed hour in recovery, I was returned to my room. By this time, Natalie and the little girls were also here. My little Miranda and "Sissy" Hannah were there to brighten my day.

My family had spoken with Dr. Olt after the surgery was finished. They told me that the lump with the tissue around it had been nearly the size of a golf ball, and that two sentinel lymph nodes had been removed. That was all I knew, except that there was no drain to contend with. No drain meant that the dissection performed had not been as extensive as I had feared in the recovery room.

I was given instructions for wound care and the follow-up appointment with my surgeon. The liver biopsy was scheduled for the following Monday.

Another Liver Biopsy

So, before I had recovered from the surgery sufficiently to lift my arm above my head again without pain, I returned to the hospital for the second liver biopsy. This one proved to be more uncomfortable than the first one had been despite the fact that I was taking more Percocet now than I'd had in several months. I had been surprised by the amount of post-operative pain I'd had.

Previously the liver biopsy had been done with an anterior approach, or from the front. This time a different Radiologist was performing the procedure, and she chose to approach laterally, from the right side. That meant that the cannula or probe through which the biopsy forceps would be passed had to be inserted *between* my ribs. With every breath I could feel it move. Furthermore, it was not in the proper spot upon the first insertion, and it was necessary to readjust its position not once, but twice. After each repositioning I would be put back into the scanner to check its position, all the while trying to measure my breaths evenly to reduce the pain involved. Finally it was in the desired location. Again I felt as though I had been stabbed!

Finally, she was able to proceed with obtaining the tissue samples. Each time I was instructed to hold my breath and I heard the 'Snap!' of the biopsy forceps as the "bites" were taken. There would be a delay of several minutes as the pathologist examined the tissue sample, then requested another. Three samples were taken in all. The procedure took nearly two hours.

All this time I had to lie very still with my arms up above my head on the table, taking only shallow breaths. (Try it. It's not easy even without an instrument stuck between your ribs!) The Radiology techs were so kind and helpful to me.

It would be a week before I knew the results.

Will the News Be Good?

We were understandably anxious that seventeenth day of October as Earl, Mom and I arrived at Dr. Powell's office. Soon he entered with my burgeoning chart. Earl made some remark about how the doctor needed a wheeled cart to carry the volume of information included there. He took his seat after greeting us and opened the chart. I could not anticipate what I was about to hear, could not read any expression on his face.

"The pathology report shows that the tumor margins were clear," he said. "And the two sentinel nodes and the six other lymph nodes that were removed were also clear."

So that explained the unexpected soreness in my armpit! They had removed eight lymph nodes instead of two as I had thought. That explained the longer surgery and the subsequent discomfort. Furthermore, as he continued, the liver biopsy had revealed *no presence of cancer cells. I was cancer free!*

This moment, for which I had longed and anticipated nearly two years, was finally here and strangely I felt no great sense of relief! I had expected this moment to be one of great joy and wild celebration. Why did I not feel it? My paranoia was showing again!

I expressed my gratitude for his patience and persistence throughout our time together during treatment and gave Dr. Powell a hug. What was missing for me? I had expected to be 'dancing-in-the-streets' happy. Why was that emotion not there?

Even as we shared the news with family and friends I was strangely reserved, still not really understanding why. Again, it all felt like a ruse, a charade. I was afraid to be too happy even with the best news we'd had in two years!

Though the last dose of chemotherapy had actually been in September, it was not until now, nearly three weeks later that I knew for sure there would be no more chemo. On the way out of the office that day it was *my* turn to ring the bell! I paused with my hand on the rope savoring the moment. Then I pulled it back and forth, hard, several times. I hoped someone in the back room getting chemo would hear it and be encouraged that *their* turn to ring the bell would come soon.

The Finish Line is in Sight!

The realization that I was really on the final leg of this marathon came several days later when I called for the results of the last blood sample that was sent off for a Tumor Marker report. Nancy, one of the lab techs that work in Dr. Powell's office was on the phone. She looked for the report and I waited, pencil poised to write on yet another sticky note.

She came back to the phone. "Dr. Powell initialed the report. It says 37."

I repeated it back to her, unable to believe what I was hearing. "Did you say 37?"

"Yes," she answered. "It's 37." The normal value for someone who does not have breast cancer is **0-38.4**. For the first time since I had *heard* of tumor markers, mine was *normal*!!

Now I felt like celebrating!! Earl would tease that it was the first thing that had **ever** been normal about me! And I didn't even mind the teasing!

I called Mom and my sisters and all four children! Finally, after 45 chemo treatments and countless days languishing in near stupor, I felt free of this disease! I called my nurse-friend Sharon, and other friends. There were so many people to inform. I e-mailed my former workmates and Jim and Mary.

All that remained was the radiation therapy. How would that be?

Chapter 21

Gettin' Some Rays!

Surgery is always followed by radiation treatments. It's a given. Just as night follows day. You almost don't have a choice. But it seems like a good system and one that has worked well for many years.

What is new is that studies have shown that the survival rate with mastectomy and radiation is not longer than the survival with lumpectomy and radiation. So, if you have a choice there... well, you have to decide for yourself. Again, everyone's situation is different. No one else can decide for you. You must be satisfied that the decision was entirely yours.

Here I Go, Thinking Again!

So, the appointment was made to see the radiation oncologist several weeks after my surgery. _My_ thinking had been that since the tumor margins had been clear and all the lymph nodes removed had been clear, perhaps I wouldn't need quite so many radiation treatments. Wrong again!

The magic number (at least for everyone I've ever known who had radiation for breast cancer) is 34. So I would be scheduled for 34 treatments. The last nine are called the "boost" treatments. It is not a larger amount of radiation, but is directed instead to a smaller area. Just the area where the tumor was.

I had seen an article in our local paper just two days prior to my visit. It described a new treatment that is being done locally, called MammoSite. While the therapy has been in use since 2002, it is new to our community.

Certain criteria must be met to have this treatment, but it involves insertion of a "balloon" in the cavity where the tumor was. Then the patient goes to the radiation center twice a day for 5 days and some radioactive material is placed in the balloon, effectively radiating just the tumor site. Five days of treatment instead of 34! I decided to ask about it.

Do I Qualify for MammoSite?

Earl and I went to the Radiation Oncology center for my meeting with Dr. Rena Zimmerman. The Radiation center is housed in a building diagonally across the street from the main hospital building. I had never been inside it before. It has a beautiful 'meditation room' that has a large water fountain with water that trickles down over large pieces of glass hanging from the ceiling. It resembles a large wind chime with the pieces horizontal instead of vertical. The sound of the water is very soothing.

Dr. Zimmerman is tall and slender with medium length brown hair. Her manner is unassuming and she has a kind, caring demeanor. We discussed my cancer history at length and chatted about mundane matters, too. I liked this woman immediately. She is so "down-to-earth."

Dr. Zimmerman talked about the MammoSite before I could ask about it. One of the criteria is that the patient must not have cancer anywhere else in the body, but I'd had a great deal of liver involvement. However, it was gone now and after some careful consideration she said, "We *could* consider that you never had it since it is not there now." She was excited at the prospect of doing this procedure on a new "class" of patients.

She ordered a CT scan to be done immediately to determine if the surgical cavity was large enough to accommodate the radiation balloon. The scan was done in another room there at the radiation center.

The resulting decision was that the cavity was large enough, but my surgeon, unaware of the new procedure or that I might qualify for it, had placed some surgical clips in the tumor site for easy location in case other tumors should appear in my breast in the future. The clips would make it possible to determine whether the tumor was in a new site or a recurrence of the old tumor. Unfortunately, this made the MammoSite impossible as the clips might rupture the balloon.

Hang On... You're Almost There!

So, back to planning the 34-treatment schedule, I went to another room where we continued the discussion. Dr. Zimmerman was amazed that I had endured 45 treatments of chemotherapy, and she said, "For our patients who have had chemo, radiation is a walk in the park."

We talked about the fact that the situation had been so grim in the beginning and appeared totally different now!

Dr. Zimmerman said, "You *know* you're a miracle!"

And when I mentioned that I tend to be a little paranoid and that I was actually fearful of coming off of treatment, she said, "Don't look a gift horse in the mouth! I used to have a partner when I worked in Arizona who would say, 'Miracles happen. Be available!' But you might want to be careful when you leave here because you may just have used up all the good luck you're going to have!"

After expressing how happy and grateful we are for the remarkable recovery, we told her also about the Florida hurricanes that went through Mom's former home and the tornado that hit Tiffin after Mark and his family moved. Feigning a serious attitude she held up her clipboard as if to begin writing and said, "Could you give me some numbers?"

We all laughed at the prospect of Dr. Zimmerman playing the lottery, and the visit was soon concluded. Again, I could not have been happier with my new doctor. I was ready for this final phase of treatment and eager to begin. The first one would be on the 10th of November.

In the next several days two molds or "cradles" were made for me to lie in during the treatments, one for the exposure of the entire right side of my chest, and one for the boost or exposure of only the tumor area. I would be coming to the radiation center every day at 1:45, excluding weekends and holidays. The final treatment would be on December 29. By the end of the year it would be finished! I never had an end date for treatments before now. It was exciting to finally know where the finish line was!

'Singing' My Way Through Radiation!

Just as having a baby removes a woman's modesty regarding medical people seeing her without being covered up, radiation therapy for breast cancer makes it ordinary (But **_only for a while!!_**) to have your chest uncovered in front of strangers. It made me very uneasy at first. I told the radiation techs I had never exposed my chest to so many people in my entire life! But they were very professional and never made me feel self-conscious.

I soon discovered that the time for radiation therapy goes much faster than chemo. We settled into a routine and the days went by quickly. The trip to and from the center each day and the time it took to change clothes before and after the treatment took more time than the actual treatment.

From the very first day of radiation, as I settled onto the table in my "cradle" and the measurements were taken, my thoughts turned to my Creator Jehovah God. I thought how grateful I was and continue to be for this remarkable turn of events in our lives. There is a song based on the Twenty-Third Psalm in our songbook, and it came to mind as the radiation techs left the room to begin the first treatment.

"JEHOVAH GOD IS MY SHEPHERD," I sang silently in my mind.

"SO WHY SHOULD I FEAR OR FRET? FOR HE WHO CARES FOR HIS SHEEP SO MUCH WILL NONE OF HIS OWN FORGET." There would be silence for a few moments as the proper settings were selected on the radiation "machinery."

"BY QUIET WATERS HE LEADS ME, MY SOUL DOES RESTORE AND BLESS." The buzzing-whirring sound would begin. It seemed to be the tone of G-sharp or A-sharp. (How would I know for sure?)

"HE GUIDES MY STEPS FOR HIS OWN NAME'S SAKE IN PATHWAYS OF RIGHTEOUSNESS. HE GUIDES MY STEPS FOR HIS OWN NAME'S SAKE IN PATHWAYS OF RIGHTEOUSNESS." The sound would continue long enough for several phrases of the song to run through my mind.

"THOUGH IN THE VALE OF DEEP SHADOW I WALK, I NEED FEAR NO HARM, FOR MY GREAT SHEPHERD IS ALWAYS NEAR; HIS STAFF KEEPS ME FROM ALARM."

I had read of other cancer patients who were actually frightened by the equipment and the noises it made. Others envisioned the radioactive rays as actually killing the awful cancer cells. I certainly felt as though I had been in the 'vale of deep shadow' but was beginning to emerge! I was not afraid.

"MY HEAD WITH OIL HE REFRESHES; MY CUP HE HAS FILLED UP WELL. HIS LOVING-KINDNESS WILL FOLLOW ME, AND E'RE IN HIS HOUSE I'LL DWELL. HIS LOVING-KINDNESS WILL FOLLOW ME, AND E'RE IN HIS HOUSE I'LL DWELL."

The huge arm of the machine would now move from the left side of my body to the right side for the second angle from which the healing rays would come. The tone of the machine would also change to about an octave below the first one as the tune continued in my mind.

"HOW WISE AND LOVING MY SHEPHERD! HIS PRAISES WITH JOY I SING. THE CHEERING NEWS OF HIS TENDER CARE TO SHEEP-LIKE ONES I WILL BRING." The day's effort would soon be done.

"HIS WORD I'LL FAITHFULLY FOLLOW, WALK CAREFULLY IN HIS WAY. MY GLORIOUS TREASURE OF SERVING HIM I'LL GRATEFULLY USE EACH DAY. MY GLORIOUS TREASURE OF SERVING HIM I'LL GRATEFULLY USE EACH DAY." And it was done.

The arm of the huge machine would retreat to the back of the room again. I would be helped to sit up, replace my gown, and off I'd go until the next day. This was too easy, I thought.

After that first day, I continued the mental exercise of singing this song to myself during each therapy session. It was comforting to me and helped me to express my gratitude to Jehovah as I recognized Him each day.

With successive exposure to the radiation my skin became slightly pink, then took on the appearance of actual sunburn. But there were never any breaks in my skin. I faithfully applied the skin moisturizer as recommended, and carefully avoided use of harsh bath soaps and other skin products.

As the days arrived for the nine "boost" treatments I was continuing to gain strength. I found that I did not need to nap every day any more, and the naps I did take were shorter. I felt like cooking again and doing some of the housework. There was more than a finish line to cross at the end of this race. It would be more like crossing into a new life.

People began to comment that I was smiling more. I hadn't even realized that my smile had no longer been a part of my appearance. But now that it's back, I hope it stays.

The Goal Is Achieved!

Remission at last!

The last mile of my marathon, it turns out, was not the most difficult. I had indeed "hit the wall" earlier, but I kept running or walking. As the finish line neared, I realized just how many "fans" I had in this race. They were all cheering me on.

"You can do it!" they shout. "You're almost there! You're doing great!"

With renewed strength I summon everything I have to finish the race. Remember, I started this race without any preconditioning.

Then I see it. The finish line is there and the banner across the top says, "**REMISSION!**" As I near the tape stretched across my path I can't believe I've come so far! I stretch out my 'Still Double-Breasted' chest and take those last few strides. I've done it!

At last the CT scan says there's nothing in the liver but scar tissue from "treated metastatic disease," there is no more cancer in my breast, and what we saw in the lungs is unchanged... perhaps only granulomas after all, something nearly everyone in northwest Ohio has! The tumor marker report now reads **23.9**, well below the normal high of 38. Most of the obvious effects of the chemo are gone and I feel better every day.

Earl no longer carries my purse and we are now sharing the laundry and kitchen chores. He's been back in his "shop" in the garage and built some spectacular new oak bookshelves that stand in our newly remodeled study. There wouldn't have been time for that even six months ago! We can't seem to stop smiling.

I Am Not Special

With all of this talk of "miracles" and gratitude I must say this: While I am more grateful than ever to Jehovah God for my recovery I do not believe that he is today performing miraculous cures on behalf of individuals. Otherwise there would be many more people getting well after facing such illness.

Instead, good people die every day. I am not more special than any of those people. We die because our common forefather Adam was disobedient to his Creator and could no longer pass on human perfection to his offspring.

The Bible book of Ecclesiastes describes it as "time and unforeseen occurrence" that befall us all. (Ecc. 9:11) I am fortunate enough to have met some remarkable people in the field of medicine, and perhaps our God Jehovah had a hand in seeing to that. Especially since I really did not want to work in Endoscopy at all when I took the job and only did it to get daytime work hours. Yet, without having had that job, I would not have known Dr. Sheikh and would not have known about Dr. Powell.

Additionally, Dr. Powell did not give up or become discouraged when others would have, and we never lost hope. We have read in the newspaper or on the Internet articles about therapies that he started me on last year that are now being touted as "the latest thing" in breast cancer treatment. He is ahead of the curve on everything and he is my medical hero!

However, I fully understand that remission is temporary. It means the cancer is gone… for now. There is no cure for this disease at this time. It's not a matter of *if* the cancer comes back or not, but *when*. So whatever time I have, I will enjoy!

Chapter 22

A Very Delicate Matter

My children should skip this chapter. Mom, too. And anyone else who knows me personally.

It concerns the delicate subject of intimate relations with one's mate.(See, it's even difficult for me to write about this in the first person.) Although I grew up in the 1960's during the American sexual revolution, I am not comfortable with speaking openly about such private matters. But those who suffer with this disease deserve to know some things.

Plainly worded, chemotherapy and its accompanying side-effect-treating drugs will most likely kill any thought of or desire for intimacy. And when, on rare occasion there is a hint of a memory of such things, it may quickly disappear or be impossible to fulfill. There are a variety of reasons for this, not the least of which is the overwhelming fatigue that is a result of chemo drugs.

If you're like me, you will think that part of your life is over forever. And if, like me, you are blessed with a loving, considerate mate, it will not be a problem. However, there is hope. The drugs will not be permanent residents of your body. At some point when the chemo is finished, your body will begin to rid itself of all traces of the poisonous chemicals that have been (hopefully) eradicating your body of all those evil, wayward cancer cells. You will be able to live a "normal" life again, if such a thing truly exists.

In the meantime, help is available. There are many publications out there to help with such problems and many other dilemmas. There is a wealth of information available through the American Cancer Society. They produce, among a host of others on every kind of cancer, a booklet titled *"Sexuality and Cancer* For the Woman Who Has Cancer and Her Partner." If it cannot be obtained at your local hospital or cancer center, you can call toll-free 1-800-ACS-2345 or visit on line at www.cancer.org. There is also a version of this booklet written for men and their own unique problems when undergoing treatment for cancer.

Another book I found to be most helpful was a book by Deborah A. Cohen called *Just Get Me Through This!* It is the most comprehensive publication in handbook form that covers everything I ever wanted to know about breast cancer. It is written in such a way that it can be referred to time and again as you move through the various treatment modalities. You will be able to quickly locate the information you wish to access, again and again.

Author Dave Balch has a chapter in his book *Cancer for Two*, called, "A Word About Sex During Chemotherapy". It's written from the caregiver's standpoint and is quite interesting.

Enough said.

Chapter 23

(Hopefully) Helpful Hints

Over the nearly two years of my treatment I have learned many things. Some were learned from reading the abundance of literature made available to cancer patients. Others were learned by trial and error. If I can save someone else the "error" part of that equation, all the better.

So, for what it's worth, try these things.

For Visits to the Doctor

If you're like most people, you remember what you want to talk about with your doctor just when you are *leaving* his office, or the next day or week! So, get yourself a small notebook to use during your entire illness. I found that one about 4x6 inches with 80-100 pages lasted nearly two years! Hopefully, you won't be in treatment that long and you'll have paper left over!

When a question comes up that is not of a critical nature, ***write it down...NOW!*** Because if you don't, the next time the doctor comes in the room, whatever you wanted to ask him/her goes right out of your thoughts! So, ask your questions and write down the answers as well. Keep the pages in the book, and you can refer to it if you forget that you asked already or don't remember the answer! (Remember Chemo-Brain?) You can also have a friend or family member write the answers down if you feel awkward about it. The doctor won't mind.

Some people suggest tape-recording your visits with the doctor. I find that notion to be a little too invasive, but if you and your doctor agree, go ahead. Just don't do it without asking his permission first.

Keeping Records

Get a larger notebook for keeping records of what's happening. For instance, you have nausea and the doctor gives you a new prescription. Write down what it is, when you took it and if it worked or not. Some people have unfavorable (though not allergic) reactions to some medications; for instance, one of the nausea medications I took caused me to have restless legs syndrome. If you don't realize that these symptoms began *after* you started taking the new prescription, your doctor won't know how to treat it. In other words, is this a new symptom entirely or a reaction to a new drug? In my case, the switch to another nausea medication stopped the restless legs problem.

You are entitled to copies of your test results. It is *your* medical record. Don't be afraid to ask for copies of CT scan results, x-rays and blood work. Even if you don't fully understand it, you'll have it if another doctor asks about it.

You need to keep track of when you take your pain medicine. I made a simple chart and marked it there so I could remember. Another method I switched to later is to simply put your day's supply of pain pills in a small bowl or pill cup. For instance, if you take your pain medicine every six hours, put four of them in a container each morning. When you look at it you'll be more likely to remember when you took it last, or at least not to take too many during the day. When they're gone for the day, you're done! Failing these methods, you could put someone else in charge of doling out your pills if you do not live alone.

Most of all, be aware of your own body and what's normal for you. We tend to accept many aches and pains as signs of aging, but if a number of abnormal things begin to pile up, take note and talk to your doctor. Maybe it's normal. Maybe not. Check it out.

For Yourself

Keep a journal. Write down how you feel, not just physically but emotionally. Write down things you enjoyed in the past and things you hope to do in the future. Keeping hope alive goes a long way toward improving your physical health! Write down things you want your family to know and how much you love them. Write about how you feel at the moment you are recording your thoughts. Happy things as well as sad things. It's very therapeutic. Even if you or no one else ever reads it again, you will feel better for having put your feelings on paper. It's like cleansing your mind of those thoughts so you can move on.

For Nausea

Much nausea can be prevented and, as stated earlier, is easier than treating it once it starts. So, ask for your doctor for medication. For mild nausea, find out what works best for you. I found that nibbling on a certain brand of tiny pretzel twists was good for keeping my stomach settled. And for about 48 hours after chemo, I ate light. Ramen noodles or noodle soup were good and not too heavy on a queasy stomach. For a little protein, cottage cheese was good for me. Find out what tastes good and stays down, and make a note of it.

If you're prone to nausea, say when you're in the car, take a small wastebasket lined with a plastic grocery bag or two (no holes!). A little forethought can save a lot of work.

A "Temperature" or a "Fever"?

It's a good idea to take your temperature from time to time, especially if you're not feeling well. I already owned an ear thermometer, and I love it. It gives a reading in about two seconds! It's important to know what *your* normal temperature is to know whether or not you have a fever.

While we're on the subject, as a nurse I have a pet peeve! The correct term for an elevated, or higher than normal, temperature is "**fever**" not "**temperature!**" (Even dead bodies have a "temperature," it's just much lower than a living person!)

Skin Care

I have three words to say about skin care- moisturize, moisturize, moisturize! It can't be stressed enough. I used to say I had enough oil in my skin to float a battleship, but those days are long gone, and chemo dries your skin out. So, a good facial moisturizer every day, a mild bath soap, and all-over body moisturizer will help. If you haven't the energy for that, employ the assistance of your husband (*He'll* enjoy that!), or get some body spray oil. It's quick and easy. And don't forget hand cream often throughout the day.

Mouth Sores

By all means, if you develop sores in your mouth from chemo, *tell your doctor!* He will tell you what to do or not do, such as what foods may aggravate it or what mouth rinse you may use to alleviate the problem. You may need a prescription.

What you might not be told is that at some point in your therapy your toothbrush may begin to feel like a Brill-O pad in your mouth! What to do?? Go, or as I did, send someone to the store for a *child's* toothbrush. They are much softer than any soft adult brush and very gentle on your tender gums. They are also smaller and you may have to brush each tooth individually, but it's worth the extra work.

Now the only problem you will have is explaining to your five-year-old child or grandchild that the "Scooby-Do" or "Princess" or "Spongebob" toothbrush is *yours* and that it is not for her or him! I had those as well as "Power Rangers" during my sore mouth phase. Recently I have been able to find adult toothbrushes that are 'extra soft.' Truthfully, they're not as much fun!

While we're on the subject of mouth care, during the time you're on chemo and susceptible to everything that comes along, don't share your tube of toothpaste with anyone... not even family members. We all have our own oral bacteria and they might be deposited on the toothbrush and transferred to the paste. Why take the chance?

Don't Lick Those Envelopes!

Someone recently told me that the companies that make envelopes have a minimum number of *insect parts* that are permitted in the glue that seals the envelopes! Yuck! Why can there be **any?** (Same goes for insect parts in peanut butter!! Double yuck!!) Besides, if the envelopes come with bills, you don't know *what* was on the hands of the person who stuffed it all in your envelope! Your immune system is down. Use tape to seal envelopes!

Lacking tape, try a sponge or wet paper towel or cloth to moisten the seal.

And while you're at it, buy self-adhesive stamps, too!

Carry your own toilet paper!

Speaking of compromised immune systems, think about public restrooms. Some of them are dangerous for healthy people! If you must use public restrooms, *carry your own toilet paper with you!*

If you need a more graphic reason, you don't know **what** was on the hands of the person who was there before you!! It's easy to roll some tissue up and stuff it in a sandwich bag to put in your pocket or purse.

And while you're at it, *don't sit right on that toilet seat!* Carry some antiseptic cloths (the kind that kill HIV and everything else) with you in another sandwich bag. Clean the seat and let it dry, or place a paper cover over it if you cannot wait for it to dry.

(Here's where I learned by **error!** It takes several days for your skin to recover from the disinfectant in those wipes!)

And invest in some disposable gloves to wear while you're doing someone else's cleaning job in that restroom. (Again, put 'em in a sandwich bag. They're good for more than sandwiches!)

I just put together a little "potty" kit that I took with me away from home: Sandwich bags with disinfectant wipes, gloves, and tissue, all in a small canvas bag and there you go! (So to speak!)

Another Bathroom Matter

Most chemotherapy leaves the body in the patient's urine or stool. This means that your toilet bowl will have dangerous chemicals in it every day for days at a time after your treatment. Remember, the nurses wear gloves and are careful not to get the chemo drugs on their hands! Scary to think that it's running in your veins but you can't touch it!

If other family members must use your bathroom, double-flush after you use the bathroom. And clean the bowl frequently.

And When Leaving Public Bathrooms

You know there are people who use the bathroom and dash out the door without washing their hands, but you're not one of them. Well, when they do this, they have *touched the doorknob or handle* that you must now touch to get out of there! (Unless some really

smart person made the door open **out.**)   Here's how to protect
yourself:

If there is a roll of paper towels in a dispenser:

Unroll your towel *first*

Turn the water on

Wash your hands thoroughly with soap, and rinse

(It's hard to do at first, but *don't turn the water off yet.*)

Get your paper towel and dry your hands

Keeping your towel in your hand, turn water off <u>with the towel</u>

Open door of restroom <u>with the towel</u>

Finally, toss the towel in the can while holding the door with
your foot or your elbow. If there are blow dryers instead of paper
towels, use a glove (if it's winter) or pull a sleeve down over your
hand to open the door. Be inventive with ways to not touch that
doorknob! (Why don't all restroom doors open *OUT*?)

If none of the above precautions can be observed, carry paper
towels, a napkin or hand sanitizer with you. It even comes in pocket
size containers. You'll need it.

Eating Out

Just how many people do you think have handled that menu?
Including the hostess who coughed or sneezed as you were being
seated! And you're going to have chips and salsa?? Get the hand
sanitizer out again!

While we're on the subject, avoid salads (much as you like them)
and other uncooked foods. You can't be sure how it was handled,
and there's that bathroom thing again. In spite of the "Employees
<u>must</u> wash their hands before returning to work!" signs, ... well,
you've seen it happen!

At Work

If you must work during your treatment regimen, be exceedingly
careful. Germs lurk everywhere! So how can you protect yourself?

There should be a staff of people who clean your workplace
regularly. But don't count on it. Be responsible for your own health
here as well.

Remember those antiseptic cloths you carry for the bathroom? They can be used for most other surfaces, too. Here are the most likely places to pick up an unwanted "bug" or two: doorknobs, telephone handsets, computer keyboards, desktops, pens, pencils, copy machines (sort of amusing... bugs multiplying on the "copy" machine!), kitchen areas, clipboards, keys (if passed from one employee to another at shift change), and when shaking hands with anyone.

Never, *never*, **_never_** put pens or pencils in your mouth. Or paper clips. Or your **_fingers!_** They all may be *loaded* with bacteria! And don't use your teeth for tools! (My kids heard that thousands of times!)

Nail Care

If your particular chemo damages your finger and toenails, be extra careful. Keep your hands out of water as much as possible. Moisture can get under the nails and makes a perfect medium for fungus to grow. Even with extreme care, this can happen, as it did to me. This means no washing dishes. Wearing gloves might help at first, but later as the nails become weaker and break easily, it's not possible to wear the gloves. I know, it's awful, but you'll get through it! (It's good for men to do dishes. It gets their hands clean!!)

There are several cream products on the market to strengthen nails. Ask your doctor if it is acceptable to use one of them.

Hair Care

It's good to use conditioner on your hair. Even if you never needed it before, your hair will probably become very dry. Everything changes during cancer treatment. So, if you <u>have</u> hair, condition it.

When You Can't Sleep

As I mentioned before, I used to get up and read, make lists, have a snack, do some scrapbooking, watch TV or write in my journal.

Here are some other suggestions:

-Try sleeping on the couch, in a recliner or a spare bed for an hour or two.

-Have a cup of warm milk or some special flavor of decaffeinated tea.

-Get a "sound" machine that plays a variety of sounds to soothe you. Or a CD player with headphones and something soothing that really doesn't have a tune you can follow. I find if I play familiar songs I become so wrapped up in the tune that I listen to it so carefully I can't sleep.

-Maybe some cold (or hot) cereal, or other comfort food. (Watch out for anything chocolate though, as it contains some caffeine and may keep you awake or upset your stomach.)

-Avoid acid-type foods such as tomato and citrus. They won't be good for you while you're on chemo anyway.

-Try a warm (not hot) bath or shower.

-Aromatherapy is good. Get a tart burner (it works with a 3-watt light bulb) and pop in a relaxing scent. Just be careful of the melted wax... don't put it near your bed. (Pass on this one if smells bother you.)

-If your doctor and your conscience allow it, have a small glass of wine. But don't lie down immediately as it can also upset your stomach if you're prone to reflux.

-Check to see if you've remembered all your medicine for the day. Cancer treatment today is about *prevention* of pain and nausea, not letting it get out of hand and then trying to cure it! Believe me, both are easier to deal with from that perspective! (So, if you have a lot of pain or nausea and vomiting, *tell your doctor.* He should either give you more medication or change the regimen and keep trying till he finds the right combination of drugs to keep you comfortable. Don't feel like a whiner unless you really do whine! Just tell him, "This isn't working for me.")

Odds and Ends

Keep a small flashlight by your bed for those late night meanderings. I once broke three toes because I ran into the foot of the bed in the dark!

Never leave home without your medicine! At least one of everything you take is a minimum. (Put them in another one of those sandwich bags you bought, if they zip close they're perfect.) Include more than one of your pain and nausea medicines if you're going to be gone for several hours. You never know about traffic or other delays. And some bottled water.

Medical Information

Make a list with the following information:
-Name
-Date of birth
-Medical conditions, all of them, including what type of cancer you have
-Medications you are taking, prescription and non-prescription, vitamins and herbal preparations, *and especially the chemo you are on!*
-Drug allergies- this means true allergic reactions; rash, hives, can't breathe, etc.
-Drug sensitivities- more like side effects that make it undesirable to use the drug; causes stomach ache, headache, dry mouth, etc.
-All the surgeries you have had, **ever**
-The names of all of your doctors and their specialty

Carry this list with you everywhere you go. Update it as your medications change. If you need to go to the hospital for any reason, **the nurses will <u>love</u> you!** They will think you are the best thing since sliced bread..., which has only been around since 1903... from the makers of Wonder Bread! (There's your trivia for the day!)

Also, if your oncologist sends you to another specialist, and it's bound to happen sooner or later, you'll have your list for that office as well. They can photocopy it. It will mean a lot less writing for you on those forms you have to fill out and, again, **the nurses will <u>love</u> you!**

Incidentally, this is a good idea for your spouse and your children as well. And it takes the need to remember all of it out of the way.

For Diversion

Get some of those WORD puzzle books. Not necessarily crossword puzzles (unless you're already good at them...otherwise you may not be able to think clearly enough due to the chemo and you could get frustrated!), but the kind that give you lists of 3-, 4-, up to 9-letter words and you have to fit them into the puzzle. Usually they start you out with a word, or you can cheat if you're desperate and look at the "key" in the back to get started. Some have number puzzles, too. Anything to keep your mind active.

Get some books to read. At the top of my list is the Bible. You may choose what ever interests you.

Have Some Fun!

Finally, does it really matter if there are half a dozen dirty dishes in the sink? Watch that baseball game with your husband or play with the kids or grandkids. Read a book or take a walk. Brush the dog or listen to some music. The dishes will get done eventually. So will the laundry and the vacuuming. Maybe someone else will do it for you and maybe it won't be done the way you would have done it. But it really doesn't matter after all!

When you have survived cancer, nothing in life looks the same again. Decide what's really important to you and what isn't, then enjoy life again.

Some Interesting Statistics

Days from first pain to remission	720
Visits to doctors	82
Doctors visited	18
Procedures performed	29
Chemotherapy treatments	45
Radiation treatments	34
Surgeries	2
Prescription drugs taken	42
Visits to Emergency Room	2
Admissions to hospital	0
Miles driven	1470
Cards received	356
Bouquets of flowers received	12
Meals delivered	175
Gifts	102
Approximate amount billed for services	$480,000
Amount paid out-of-pocket	$8,970
Value of Hugs, kisses and warm wishes	Priceless!!

A Shopping List

For Cleaning

Disposable gloves
'Anti-Everything' Surface
   cleaning cloths
Liquid Hand sanitizer

"Potty" Bag ☺

Zip-Close sandwich bags
Paper toilet seat covers
Toilet paper
Cloth or canvas bag to
   Carry these items

For Record Keeping

Small notebook for pocket or purse
Larger, loose-leave notebook for:
   Home 'charts'
   Copies of tests and procedures
   EOB's from insurance company
A journal and pen
Box (or drawer) for record storage

For Radiation Therapy

Liquid baby bath (I <u>love</u> Baby Magic)
Skin cream (not lotion), such as
   Cetaphil

Other

'Sound' machine, if possible, or
   soothing CD's or tapes
A good thermometer

This list was Christy's idea!

Poetry

Over the years I have written a number of poems. Some of them are included here. There is one for each of my children, and an additional one that was written about a small, mud-caked pair of our son's shoes, which I found in a dresser drawer while I was cleaning one day.

If you've read most of what precedes this, you will be somewhat familiar with the names mentioned in the poetry. The exceptions are Earl's parents, Ralph (called 'Pop' by his children) and Myrtle Fisher, who died in 1977 and 1991 respectively. We miss them terribly, along with my father, who died in 1983.

My first effort was "The Everlasting Love," written on the occasion of our 31st wedding anniversary.

The poetry 'bug' has bitten Earl several times, too. So I am including a couple of his poems that are especially meaningful to me. His variation on "Roses are red…" is such a treasure!

I have placed his poetry first.

Earl's Poetry

Together

Life together began when we were still brand new,
That we would travel life's road together no one ever knew.
In the early days we were good friends and so much time we spent,
I didn't realize this was the love of my life and that she had been sent,
To bring me love and happiness and special gifts of love,
Yes, now I now you truly are a gift,
A gift of our dear God, sent from up above.
     By Earl Fisher 11/9/04

Like most people, Earl has never been particularly eager to know a lot about the details of surgical procedures. And having only had one surgery in his life, a tonsillectomy at about age six, he tends to be disinterested in (and perhaps a little squeamish about) seeing surgical scars. Especially new ones. That said, you could understand why I was hesitant about how he would react to my surgery. Now you know why this particular verse means so much to me.

The following was attached to a gift on our Fortieth Anniversary. If you follow the 'traditional' gift suggestions, the fortieth is ruby. So the gift was a ruby necklace and earrings.

ROSES ARE RED,
AND SO ARE RUBIES.
I WOULD STILL LOVE YOU,
EVEN IF YOU HAD <u>NO</u> BOOBIES!
     By Earl Fisher 1/22/06

(Isn't that priceless!!)

The Everlasting Love

We can't remember when we met, it was so long ago.
Why we were surely babes in arms and couldn't even know
That a wish made once in passing would one day come to be,
And an Everlasting Love would come from friends like you and me.

A fifth child now was coming to the Fishers down the street,
Who had already boys and girls, and thought a girl'd be sweet.
But Mel and Bernice wanted then a bouncing baby boy,
And figured with their own two girls that they would find some joy.

And so the parents waited, watching spring and summer fly,
Each having dreams about the child, each watching time go by.
But when October rolled around and leaves began to swirl,
A boy came to the Fisher house and Melvin got a girl.

One of those parents, as a joke, asked if they'd like to trade!
They had a laugh and went their way, forgot the offer made.
They couldn't know that decades hence we two would have plans made.
We'd forge an Everlasting Love that time would never fade.

Now growing up so close as friends, these two- the boy, the girl-
We played together every day, and thus the years unfurled.
I made him play with dolls sometimes. He taught me how to bat!
I was his army buddy then, and never minded that.

We made mud "pies" and ate saltines, and, yes, green apples, too.
"But wait! Earl, isn't that your mother calling you?"
"Oh, no," he'd say, as he played on. He didn't want to leave.
Could he at that early age have something 'up his sleeve?'

Once we performed a circus. He flew right through a chair!
We swam, rode bikes, took walks, flew kites. Why, we went
everywhere!
We climbed up in the apple tree and sometimes there just sat.
And one time when I almost fell, he saved my life from that!

Throughout the years our friendship stayed a constant in our lives.
Not always close, but never far. Hey- now he even drives!
A Mercury- a '49- she really was a beaut!
With fenderskirts and white-wall tires. He really made her scoot!

He asked me to the Junior Prom. (We went in Pop's Bel-Aire.)
It really was the greatest night with everybody there.
We danced and bowled and had a snack, played Bingo 'til the end.
And when breakfast was over, we still were just good friends.

I went to school in Lima. He worked at dif'rent things.
I learned to take a temperature and other nurse-like things.
He pumped some gas and drilled for oil; he joined the National Guard.
And every now and then, it seemed, he'd see me in the yard.

And then upon a summer's eve, the year was '64,
He asked me for a date one night, and then came back for more!
We felt at ease together, not needing to impress
Each other with some witty barbs. There really was no stress.

And so the two got married, Ralph's boy and Mel's girl,
And in effect the trade was done, Ralph's Cheryl and Mel's Earl!
So now it seems incredible, as we watch the years go by,
We have four delightful children who made the time just fly.

The first to come was Angie, so articulate and sweet,
And then along came Christy, charming everyone we'd meet.
Then Mark arrived, the third child, of our lives he's the 'sonshine.'
And number four is Sarah, keeps us laughing all the time.

The years pass by so quickly now, I pick up no more toys,
Except for when those grandsons come. They're such amazing boys!
We never really know, of course, what else life has in store,
But never in these 31 years could I have asked for more.

Our Love is Everlasting and each year, more sure of that,
We work through each and every trial and never have a spat.
Retirement is an option now, in just a few more years,
But if we leave Ohio, it won't be without tears.

You see, this thing with parents, having children near their hearts,
It doesn't end when they grow up. It's really just a start!
And all the joy of raising them will never go away,
It's there locked up in memories, just for a rainy day.

We also have another hope, on which our hearts can dwell,
That through our faith and hope in God, Everlasting is, as well.
It is that life will never end, and so the bond, you see,
Can be an Everlasting Love between us- you and me.

Cheryl Fisher 1/22/97

ANGIE

She was born at ten minutes till midnight
One Sunday in hot mid-July,
Weighing seven pounds fourteen ounces,
All our time she would soon occupy.

"All babies are ugly," he'd said once,
"They're wrinkled and skinny and red."
But when it was his that he looked at,
"She sure is pretty!" he said.

She captured his heart in an instant,
With Mom's and grandparents' as well.
Her giggles delighted everyone,
She had us in her spell.

She begged "peebies" from all who came here,
Put each one in her bank with a kiss,
"By the book" she progressed through her childhood,
Except when it came to this...

It was bedtime she couldn't comply with,
Though we always resisted her plea,
Late at night she'd be just 'round the corner
Hunkered down there still watching TV!

She decided to stay up all night once,
Thought that would be such a delight,
But then changed her mind pretty quickly
When her daddy turned out the light.

As her siblings arrived in the household
Each one she would quickly embrace.
But as they grew up they would all learn
They'd better stay out of her space.

In school she was such a good student,
She fairly flew through the grades.
To the family name she brought honor,
And was given the due accolades.

Many years have passed by since that Sunday.
She's earned an Associate Degree.
And with Steve by her side she's been happy
To make a grandmother of me!

By Cheryl Fisher   June 1998

Christy

My darling daughter, number two,
Came in November, right on cue,
Followed where her sister stepped,
A secret in her heart she kept.

With strawberry curls and eyes so blue,
Her hair barrettes would sit askew,
And Thumbellina by her cheek,
They were inseparable, unique.

Her early years were so enchanted
Her heart's desire already planted.
It started with her dolls, you see,
This early "Mom" proclivity.

So when Mark came upon the scene
No happier could she have been.
She had the opportunity
To practice bein' a mom, like me.

Then Sarah came, and after school,
Although it broke a family rule,
She'd wake that baby from her nap
To play again upon her lap.

She'd make up games and play all day,

And when the toys were put away
She'd take them in her bed to sleep
Her stuffed toys all piled in a heap.

She married then, at twenty-five,
And hoped her turn would soon arrive.
And then the doctor said, "It's true,
The newest Mom will soon be you!"

Enduring much, she was so sick,
We prayed the time would pass by quick.
She finally had a babe to love!
And thanked our Father up above.

I know as Mom she will excel,
She's kind and sensitive, as well.
As wisdom she works to amass
My feeble efforts she'll surpass.

My motherhood I would not trade
Despite mistakes that I have made.
Without it I'd not be complete,
Life wouldn't have been half as sweet.

To tell the truth I'm not so great,
I'm often wrong and overweight.
Mom's don't come with a guarantee,
They only love their family.   By Cheryl S. Fisher June 1998

Little Brown Shoes

In the top drawer of his dresser is a pair of little shoes,
Once placed upon some little feet, now treasured, not to lose.
They carried 'round those little feet upon his pride and joy,
The feet belonged to #3, his only little boy.

They took the boy, as he would play all over his back yard,
But not alone, as always he had sisters standing guard.
And when he dressed up in his suit, going to the Kingdom Hall,
Dad cleaned those shoes until there was no dirt on them at all.

The shoes were soon too small for him. Our children grow so fast.
And to the store we went to find replacement shoes at last.
The ones we chose were sneakers, all sturdy, bright, and neat.
But not for him. He didn't want "those 'neakers" on his feet!

We said, "But these are really cool!" The boy still held his ground.
They weren't brown and would not work to carry him around.
And then we thought about an ad. It said, "Go-faster Keds!."
For though the brand was not the same, the thought now filled our heads.

"With these shoes on you'll have more grip to run, and really fast!"
And so the need for only brown was something in the past.
True to our word, the sneakers worked. The boy ran everywhere.
And soon those, too, would be worn out and he'd be unaware

That in Dad's dresser at the top those little brown shoes stayed,
Still caked with mud from when the boy inside those shoes had played.
He takes them out and holds them close remembering wistfully
The precious boy whose feet produced a full-blown symphony.
(He had "muzak" in his feet!)

So many shoes have come and gone each time in larger sizes,
And though he knew that it would come, he hardly recognizes
The little boy who wore the shoes, for now he is a man.
He couldn't think that far ahead when this boy's life began.

The boy now wears his father's shoes, no, not the self-same pair,
They'd never fit, he's grown so much. But now he has an heir!
So he, too, wears a father's shoes, and being like his dad,
Someday he'll have some little shoes that make him almost sad.

In the top drawer of his dresser is where he'll store them, too.
He'll think about those little feet and how the time just flew.
And so his mem'ries coincide, and make his heart to burst,
With those of his own father, who treasured his shoes first.

By Cheryl S. Fisher   July, 2000

Above left, Hannah, Miranda, and Zach Fisher; right, Dillyn; and
below, Baby Ryleigh.   Being Fishers, the three new children are
all additions to Mark's family.

Sarah

She came here all red-faced and chubby,
As child number four, took her place.
And, like all the others before her,
Has stolen our hearts with grace.

The name that we gave her is Sarah,
In Hebrew it means "Princess,"
And now that she's grown to such beauty
Just how could we treat her as less?

She's always been awed by discoveries
Of beauty in life all around,
And once said, when a toddler, as doves cooed,
"Now that's a comfortable sound!"

Her closest and constant companion
Was big brother, Mark. What a pair!
But my did she ever object
When he caught Hot Wheels cars in her hair!

They played, ate, and slept near each other,
Never more than an arms-length apart,
Each one looking out for the other
As though they knew in their hearts,

That one day they'd be separated
By distance and miles, but still near,
Keeping close in touch on the phone now
Their bond remains sincere.

She soon became her own person,
In school learned to sing and dance,
And charmed us all with her laughter
As though we were in a trance!

So soon she was grown up and lovely,
With straight teeth and natural curls,
And sweet as ice cream in summer,
Just like our other two girls.

And now, as the last child at home here
She's learning to make her way,
Charming all sorts of men on the airwaves
With her witty tête-à-tête.

We know the day is approaching,
Though she came here all red-faced and chubby,
When she'll be leaving here quite a young lady,
With her tall and handsome hubby!

By Cheryl S. Fisher
  June 1998

Cancer Survivor

I used to wonder how I might react
If I were ever given the fact
That life as I knew it might soon be cut short.
What would I do with news of that sort?

It happened six weeks into 2004.
I tried to work on just a few days more.
Breast cancer, already in liver and chest,
What would we do now to make our chances best?

Once it all was confirmed
We'd not sit 'round and mope.
We assembled our team
At the Center of Hope.

Dr. Powell's at the helm heading up the whole crew,
With Cherie, Katina and Vickie, too.
Nancy and Stacey do lab work with care,
While appointments are scheduled from Judy's chair.

My right arm of strength is my husband so dear,
Followed closely by Angie and Christy, now here,
Then Sarah, and Mark who took charge of their fear,
And Mom and my sisters- they all bring me cheer.

Our dear Friends are faithful, too numerous to name,
And friends by the score from that job who all came,
Sharing warm greetings, their food and their hugs,
Staying away when the job gives them "bugs"!

But the hope that's the strongest is not new to me,
It's my faith in Jehovah, God of eternity.
His promise is sure, one I firmly believe,
That He'll hold my hand while I smile or I grieve.

So, how's it going nine months since that day?
Is all that old Cancer going away?
Blood work says, "Yes!" Tumor Markers near norm.
We have been able to weather this storm!

Hair's fallen out, all the nails have gone bad.
Food has no taste. Many think that's too sad.
But I'm able to be with my family each day.
I'm mostly pain-free. Side effects go away.

How much longer this takes no one knows here on earth,
All we know is we're waiting for that word of great worth,
The one that's the center of everyone's mission,
We're waiting to hear, "Cheryl, you're now in remission!"

"Your chemo is over. Go out. Ring the bell!
Then tell friends and family you'll soon feel quite well."
And, thanks Dr. P, for giving me time
To compose and record for you this little rhyme.

By Cheryl Fisher 11/25/2004

The Bell

I passed it by
Each time I came,
Week after week
It looked the same.

I'd greet the nurses,
See the doc,
They'd start the drugs,
I'd watch the clock.

Month after month
That's how it went.
Come in, go out,
Though I was spent.

But now and then
Above the noise,
I'd hear the bell
And share their joys.

Someone is done,
Their chemo's through!
And one day soon
Mine will be, too.

I'll grab that rope
And yank it hard,
It will be heard
Out in the yard!

**I rang the bell on
October 17, 2005!**

And someone sitting in a chair,
(Perhaps someone with no more hair)
Will hear the bell and they'll have hope
That one day too, they'll pull the rope.

The treatments over,
Now we can
Move on.

By Cheryl S. Fisher 9/30/2005

Suggested Reading List

A Breast Cancer Journey, Your Personal Guidebook, Second Edition, 2004, from the Experts at the American Cancer Society.

Bodai, Ernie M.D. and Zmuda, Richard, *"I Flunked My Mammogram;"* 2005, B2Z Publishing, Severna Park, Maryland, 21146.

Balsh, Dave, *Cancer for Two,* 2003, Published by A Few Good People, Inc., Twin Peaks, California, 92391.

Cohen, Deborah A. with Gelfand, Robert M., M.D., *Just Get Me Through This!;* 2000, Kensington Publishing Corporation, New York, NY, 10022.

Fiore, Neil A. Ph.D., *The Road Back to Health, Coping with the Emotional Aspects of Cancer,* 1990, Celestial Arts, Berkeley, CA, 94707.

Frahm, Anne E. with Frahm, David J., *A Cancer Battle Plan;* 1992 Pinion Press, Colorado Springs, CO, 80935.

Roberts, Steven R., *Twenty-Nine Months, A Fifteen-Year Fight with Cancer and its Consequences,* 2005, S.R. Productions Publishing, Dearborn, MI, 48120.

Sorenson, Sharon and Metzger, Suzanne, *The Complete Idiot's Guide to Living with Breast Cancer;* 2000, Alpha Books, New York, NY, 10014.

Weiss, Marisa C., M.D., and Weiss, Ellen; *Living Beyond Breast Cancer,* 1998, Three Rivers Press, New York, NY.

Web sites of interest:

www.cancer.org - The American Cancer Society, a nationwide community-based voluntary health organization that provides booklets, brochures and many other services for those involved with this disease.

www.komen.org - The Susan B. Komen website, open forum, questions & answers.

www.lbbc.org - Living Beyond Breast Cancer

www.menagainstbreastcancer.org - website for husbands, fathers, brothers of breast cancer patients, helpful with how caregivers can cope, and how to be of assistance to their loved ones

www.thebreastcancersite.com - One click a day can help fund mammograms for those who can't afford them. Also a fun place to shop!

Note from the Author: The information available with a minimal search can be mind-boggling. I wanted to understand what was out there for me in the way of treatment options, but had neither the desire nor the physical ability to examine much of it. I selected what seemed to be best for me and some of those reference works are listed here. Please visit your local library, the library in your local hospital, women's center or radiation center, and the American Cancer Society for more information. Not only does it help you to see that others have coped successfully with this illness, but their stories will give you courage. There is nearly always someone who has had a worse time than we have had, and her (or his) hope spurs us on!

Credits

Quotes from songs from *Sing Praises to Jehovah*, 1984, Watch Tower Bible and Tract Society of Pennsylvania, Brooklyn, New York.

> Song Number 48, "Give Jehovah the Praise"
> Song Number 55, "Daily Walking With Jehovah"
> Song Number 77, "Jehovah Is My Shepherd"

Cover art by Sarah Smith

Photos by Cheryl Fisher and Sarah Smith.

Poems by Earl Fisher and Cheryl Fisher.

Postscript   August 2010

I am now approaching 4 years in remission and have enjoyed 6 ½ years as a survivor. I still put my eyebrows on every day as I have never grown back more than half of what I had. The lashes are also few in number. My hair is still thin in places. None of this bothers me like it once would have.

In October of 2006 I had another surgery to biopsy the right lung. A wedge resection was also done. No cancer cells were found, so I have a clean bill of health from there, too!

Earl and I have been able to travel more and have seen the Grand Canyon and the Pacific coast, including the California redwoods.

We have also added a grandson, Zachary James Fisher, and two more granddaughters, Dillyn Xanthe and Ryleigh Sue Fisher, to our family.

Life is good!